THE ECONOMY OF BANGLADESH

The Economy of Bangladesh

AZIZUR RAHMAN KHAN

Macmillan

St. Martin's Press

First published 1972 by
THE MACMILLAN PRESS LTD
London and Basingstoke
Associated companies in New York Toronto
Dublin Melbourne Johannesburg and Madras

Library of Congress catalog card no. 72–88005

SBN 333 14546 1 730l

Printed in Great Britain by
WESTERN PRINTING SERVICES LTD
Bristol

DR

330.95492

20 NOV 1972

TO AUBHIK AND DIBBO

in the hope that by the time they grow up to be able to read this book the description of Bangladesh in the following pages will have become part of prehistory

Contents

Contents   ix

Preface

THIS book has been written in a great hurry. Although it incorporates the results of research undertaken by me and a large number of other economists over many years, the actual writing was done between the New Year and Easter of 1972. Without the help and encouragement received from many friends and colleagues, it would have been impossible to complete the work in such a short time.

I am particularly indebted to Keith Griffin, Hasan Imam and James Mirrlees. Dr Griffin provided badly-needed encouragement in the early days of writing. I profited greatly from the constant exchange of ideas with him during the summer of 1971 when we were jointly preparing *Growth and Inequality in Pakistan*. He also made countless editorial improvements in the final draft of the manuscript. Dr Imam took great care in reading through an earlier draft and suggesting improvements. My debt to Professor Mirrlees is much wider than is acknowledged in Chapter 10. I have greatly benefited from the many discussions I had with him on the various themes presented in the book.

Daniel Thorner read parts of the manuscript and made suggestions which proved extremely valuable. At Nuffield College I was able to discuss many of the issues with Ian Little, Maurice Scott, Max Corden and other members of the College. In a wider sense, the present work owes a great deal to my colleagues at the Bangladesh (formerly Pakistan) Institute of Development Economics. My thoughts have been influenced by those of the many other members of staff at the Institute over years of close contact. I am also very grateful to my brother, Lutfur Rahman Khan, who has been the Registrar of the Co-operative Societies in Bangladesh since 1969. He not only kept encouraging me to write such a book but was of immense help in finding various materials on rural Bangladesh.

The book was written during the last months of my stay at Nuffield College as a Senior Research Fellow. It is my pleasant duty to thank the Warden and the Fellows of the College for the numerous facilities so generously provided.

My wife helped in a number of ways, especially with proof-reading at various stages. I owe her sincere gratitude for this help and deep apology for the numerous consequences of the pressure of intensive work during the months of writing. Finally, I must thank Mr Alauddin Talukder for all the trouble he has taken in preparing the index.

Nuffield College   A. R. K.
Oxford
April 1972

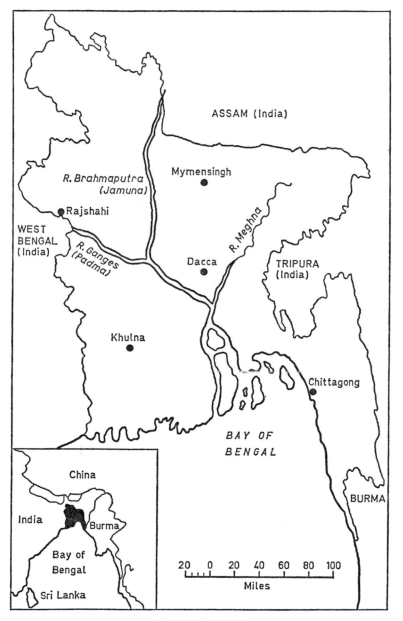

ASSAM (India)

R. Brahmaputra
(Jamuna)

Mymensingh

Rajshahi

WEST
BENGAL
(India)

R. Ganges
(Padma)

R. Meghna

Dacca

TRIPURA
(India)

Khulna

Chittagong

BAY OF
BENGAL

BURMA

China

India

Burma

Bay of
Bengal

Sri Lanka

20   0   20   40   60   80   100

Miles

BANGLADESH

Some Basic Facts

Area   55,126 square miles

Estimated population   72 million, of whom 81 per cent are Muslims

Location   Between 20° 30' and 27° N., and between 88° and 93° E. approximately

Physical features   Except for some mountainous regions in the east and south-east, the whole country is deltaic plain

Rainfall   Between 55 in. in the west and 200 in. in the east, concentrated during the five monsoon months between mid-May and mid-October

Temperature   Mean of maximum, 88°; mean of minimum, 70° F. Maximum recorded temperature, 105°; minimum recorded temperature, 38° F.

Chronology of Political Events

1947 The contiguous Muslim majority parts of the British Indian provinces of Bengal and Assam are carved out to form the province of East Bengal, which is united with the geographically separated Muslim provinces of the north-western part of British India in a federal Muslim state called Pakistan.

1954 The United Front of the opposition parties, demanding maximum regional autonomy for East Bengal among other things, defeats the ruling Muslim League by capturing 97 per cent of the seats in the first elections to the provincial legislature. The United Front Government is dismissed within weeks of assuming power by the Central Pakistan Government on the pretext of anti-national attitudes.

1956 The first Constitution of Pakistan is adopted, forming a highly centralised federation between East Bengal (renamed East Pakistan) and the provinces of West Pakistan (soon afterwards unified into one province). East Pakistan is given fewer representatives per head of electorate in the National Assembly than West Pakistan.

1958 Scheduled national elections are cancelled. General Ayub Khan takes power through a military coup and imposes a virtually unitary form of government giving the authoritarian Central Government the power to appoint and dismiss the Provincial Government, which was not responsible to the legislature elected on the basis of very limited franchise.

1966 Sheikh Mujibur Rahman of the Awami League demands the autonomy of East Pakistan on the basis of a six-point programme which envisaged a central government with responsibilities for defence and foreign affairs only while giving all taxation and economic powers to the provincial governments.

1968 The Pakistan Government attempts to crush the autonomy movement by instituting a conspiracy trial against
Sheikh and others.

1969 Nationwide political upsurge topples Ayub Khan, who is
succeeded by General Yahya Khan. The latter promises
elections to transfer power to the popular representatives.

1970 Sheikh's Awami League wins a massive election victory in
December, capturing all but two seats in the National
Assembly from East Pakistan.

1971 On 25–6 March the Pakistan Army cracks down on the
autonomist forces who were demanding immediate transfer of power to the elected party in East Pakistan on the
basis of complete regional autonomy. Mass killing and
destruction in Dacca and elsewhere in East Pakistan
follow the arrest of Sheikh by the army. The Government
of the People's Republic of Bangladesh is proclaimed in
April by the nationalist resistance led by the Awami
League and spearheaded by the rebellious Bengalis in the
Pakistan army.[1] India provides sanctuary to Bangladesh
guerillas. Tension builds up between India and Pakistan
leading to the outbreak of full-scale war in early December. The joint Indian and Bangladesh Command accepts
the surrender of the Pakistan army in Dacca on 16
December 1971.

1972 Bangladesh is recognised by most European and Asian
countries by February. Indian army withdrawal from
Bangladesh completed on 12 March.

[1] 'Bangladesh' is the traditional local-language name of the linguistic
area consisting of the present state of Bangladesh and the present Indian
state of West Bengal.

List of Tables

PART I

Population and Standard of Living

1 Introduction

THE year 1971 has seen the emergence of Bangladesh as the eighth largest nation on earth. Indeed it marked the creation of the largest nation in the quarter-century since the partition of the Indian subcontinent. There is, naturally, a great deal of curiosity about the new-born nation. The world seems to be trying, without much success to date, to make up its mind about the possibilities of this nation. Is it likely to become a viable and independent nation capable of coping not only with the massive short-term problems of refugee rehabilitation and economic reconstruction but also with the long-run ones of combating the extremes of poverty, hunger, disease and illiteracy?

A sensitive observer can hardly fail to identify the positive and negative circumstances of the emergence of the new nation. More than any other nation of comparable or larger size, Bangladesh has remarkable linguistic, ethnic and cultural homogeneity. A single language, with a single script and a reasonably developed literature, is spoken by almost all the people. Except for a minute proportion of border tribesmen, the whole population is remarkably similar in cultural habits. Religion, the most outstanding source of rivalry among people on the Indian subcontinent, has almost totally been in the background for quite some time and, barring a major mistake by the political leadership, is unlikely to surface again as a dominant factor. Internally, there seems to be few vested interest groups strong enough to take a resolute stand against social reform. Feudal interests, though still in existence and dominant in rural production relations, are nowhere near the Latin-American or Middle-Eastern latifundias in size, power or political influence. Domestic capitalists, completely dominated by their West Pakistani counterparts in the past, would not be strong enough to impose their will on a determined government to persuade it to adopt an industrialisation policy which benefits them at the cost of national welfare. In view of the circumstances of its creation and the geopolitical realities, a sensible political leadership can do away with the need of having a large army, thereby eliminating another wasteful claim on resources, so frequently proving a major stumbling block to economic growth in the subcontinent.

As a counterbalance to these positive factors there would appear to be some negative economic ones, which are being strongly emphasised by the many critical observers of Bangladesh. Bangladesh is a massive concentration of extreme poverty which defies comparison. Nowhere on earth is there anything like such extremely low living standards shared by such an enormous mass of population squeezed into so small a geographical area. Just as great or even greater poverty may perhaps be found in parts of Asia, e.g. in Afghanistan, in parts of India or in East Indies; but such cases are small pockets of at most a few millions compared with the 72 millions in Bangladesh.

What appears to be even more discouraging to the eyes of a conventional economist is the lack of any obvious source of large surplus. In many Asian countries, characterised by massive poverty, there are to be found pockets of abundance, e.g. in the extremely high consumption of a handful of landed aristocrats and perhaps also traders. In such economies sensible social and economic reforms hold out the promise of large surplus generation which could lead to rapid growth. In Bangladesh, thanks to the land reforms of early 1950s, there seems to be relatively little elbow room.

Compounding all these difficulties are the circumstances of the emergence of the nation: the dislocation and damage to the economic overheads during the nine-month war and the extraordinarily massive claim on resources for the rehabilitation of the ten million refugees.

The question of the viability of Bangladesh is, therefore, a complicated one. The answer depends on the careful balancing of the favourable and unfavourable objective conditions and the evaluation of the possibilities of the subjective factors, e.g. the resilience of the society and its leadership and their capacity to absorb shocks. The purpose of the present study is to highlight the economic aspects of the question. It begins by analysing the existing structure of the economy with the objective of identifying the main problems. This seems to be important in itself.

There is a great deal of confusion today in the characterisation of what the economy is like and which problems are the important ones. From the description of the existing reality, an attempt is made to define social priorities and explore the policies that would ensure their achievement.

Throughout the present work, emphasis is placed on quantification. Both the existing structure and the future possibilities are quantified even when it amounts to pushing the frontier of statistical knowledge rather hard. Although there are important gaps in such knowledge, a good deal of quantitative information can be assembled with only moderately sustained effort.

Part I of the study tries to establish some of the demographic characteristics and examines in detail the current standard of living with some analysis of its change over the last two decades. Part II presents an analytical description of the structure of the Bangladesh economy today. Major productive sectors and the overall resources are evaluated with a view to identifying the important characteristics and problems. Part III looks at the future, beginning with the application of a model to identify the overall priorities and to quantify various scarcities, and going on to discuss the future profiles of the major sectors and examine the resource balance.

2 Population and Labour Force

2.1 POPULATION SIZE AND DENSITY

BECAUSE of the circumstances of the independence of Bangladesh, it is rather difficult to be sure of a benchmark population figure. First, the decennial population census which was due to be taken early in 1971 could not be held because of the political situation. Thus the population estimates of today are more than ever removed from the most recent year of count. Any small margin of error in the estimated growth rates over the last decade would by now have cumulated into a large error. Secondly, the year 1971 in Bangladesh witnessed what probably was the largest demographic disturbance over the whole history of mankind. An estimated ten million people were driven out of Bangladesh through a reign of terror. It is, at the very least, hazardous to try to project population in future until the vast number of transients settle down.

In this situation, it seems best to try to obtain a benchmark population estimate at, say, January 1971, which is an immediate pre-turmoil date. As we have already pointed out, this is far from easy in view of the last census being a decade old. The redeeming factor, however, consists of the consistent and systematic efforts during the 1960s to establish various demographic rates through the Population Growth Estimates (PGE) Survey launched by the Central Statistical Office[1] and the then Pakistan (now renamed Bangladesh) Institute of Development Economics (BIDE).

To get a reasonable estimate of population in recent years, it is necessary to have a firm estimate for the year of the last census (January 1961). Demographers at the Pakistan Institute of Development Economics, after a careful comparison of the census sex and age distribution with that of the more reliable

[1] References to the CSO and the Planning Commission are to the pre-1971 Pakistan agencies of same names. The references to the comparable Bangladesh agencies are made explicit.

PGE, made detailed corrections for the various sex and age groups.[1] Their adjusted figure of 53·4 million seems to be a reliable estimate for the mid-fiscal year 1960/61. These demographers then made alternative projections for the next forty years using alternative assumptions with respect to age and sex specific fertility rates. These assumptions are based on alternative interpretations of the PGE and evaluations of the possibilities of government action. The projection that seems most reasonable to us for the decade of the sixties is based on the assumption that overall crude birth rate, reaching a peak of about 55 per thousand in 1965, will thenceforward begin an annual decline of about 1·3 per thousand. This is consistent with the findings of both the PGE and the preliminary evaluations of the family planning programme.

The above projection provides us with a July 1970 population estimate of 71·5 million. Adding half-yearly growth of 1·5 per cent we arrive at a January 1971 (i.e. mid-fiscal year 1970/71) estimate of 72·6 million. Allowing for the unprecedented cyclone toll of November 1970, we should be making as close an estimate for January 1971 as is possible by putting the figure at 72 million.[2]

Total population may have declined to something between

[1] Bean, L. L., M. R. Khan and A. R. Rukanuddin, *Population Projections for Pakistan 1960–2000* (Karachi 1968).

[2] It may be mentioned that this estimate is almost identical with the one that could be obtained by updating by a growth rate of 3 per cent the series that the Planning Commission was using until recently. The latest Planning Commission series is slightly higher and the CSO series slightly lower than our estimate. The accusation of underestimation will be made by those who believe that by mid-1969 population had reached 72 million (e.g. the U.S. Bureau of Census). This, however, seems too high. To accept such a high figure, either one has to settle for a higher benchmark figure for the last census date or accept an annual compound rate of growth significantly higher than 3 per cent. There does not seem to be any compelling argument in favour of either. Finally, it appears to the present author that the result of the 1971 Indian Census goes to some extent to disprove the extremely pessimistic projections that had been proliferating in recent demographic studies. After all, the projections since 1960 are based on much higher rates of growth than were observed during the preceding inter-censal decade. Such high rates needed to be confirmed by actual count. The first evidence, for India, shows that the actual rate has been lower. Our figure, however, should only be taken as an estimate with a significant possible margin of error.

62 and 63 million by December 1971 owing to the exodus of the refugees to India. By January 1972, refugees had started trickling back to independent Bangladesh and it seems likely that most will have returned by the end of fiscal 1971/72. And yet population by July 1972 may not be much higher than it was in January 1971 owing to the massive killing in the war, the more than average death rate among the refugees, the emigration of some non-Bengali minorities and the possible decline of the birth and survival rates due to the unprecedented dislocation in families. In most calculations below, we shall simply use the 1971 benchmark population as this is our best estimate not only of the pre-war population but also of the population by the end of the present transitory phase.

Urban population in 1961 was only 5·19 per cent of the total. Since 1961, the rate of urbanisation has certainly been more rapid than the overall population growth although there is no direct statistical basis for a firm numerical estimate. We can hardly do better than look at past trends. Between the 1951 and 1961 decennial censuses, the annual rate of growth of the twenty biggest towns was 1·73 times higher than that for the population as a whole. The bigger towns probably grew faster than the smaller ones, but so probably did the urban areas during the sixties as compared to the fifties. Using 1·73 as the elasticity of urbanisation with respect to population we arrive at a 1971 urban population estimate of 4·7 million which is only 6·5 per cent of total population. Thus even by the subcontinental standards, Bangladesh is overwhelmingly rural.

2.2 LABOUR FORCE

In a country like Bangladesh, the definition of labour force itself is difficult. Still its measurement is made mainly to quantify the gap between labour supply and actual employment to derive some quantitative idea of the extent of 'surplus labour' and the urgency of employment creation. Where a good deal of employment is mere work-sharing or 'disguised unemployment', such measurements are necessarily imprecise.[1] The following

[1] Also labour supply itself is a somewhat elastic concept as can be seen from the examination of the criteria of minimum age. A 12-year-old in an Asian village without any facilities for schooling seems to be a justified

numerical estimates should be interpreted subject to such qualifications.

The CSO estimated the urban and rural participation rates in Bangladesh to be respectively 35·27 per cent and 34·44 per cent for 1966/67.[1] Using these rates for 1970/71 we get labour force estimates of 1·64 million and 23·20 million respectively for urban and rural areas. While arguments can be found on both sides regarding the accuracy of such labour force estimates, it would appear that these participation rates, used in conjunction with the population growth rates, would be reasonable indicators of incremental employment requirement.[2] These rates will undoubtedly change in future, but there is too much uncertainty to make predictions of such change worthwhile. With the spread of primary and secondary education, the rates would tend to decline. In the long run this would certainly be greatly outweighed by changes in age composition of population (brought about by changing patterns of fertility and mortality) and the status of women. What happens in the near future will depend on which transition precedes which.

inclusion while a 15-year-old in Western-Europe, with compulsory schooling is not.

[1] CSO, *Summary of Population and Labour Force (July 1966–June 1967)*, Report of a Survey (mimeographed).

[2] The CSO defines labour force to include non-institutional population of 10 years of age or above who were *found employed* or looking for employment, but to exclude agricultural and other property owners and those engaged in 'immoral pursuits' (including, somewhat surprisingly, beggars). To the extent no society should want its 10-year-olds to work for a living, the estimate might be biased upward. It is doubtful, however, that many parents in the survey actually enumerated such children as looking for employment. A comparison of the frequency distribution of the age of population shows that even after allowing for an extremely low female participation rate (about 15 per cent of the rural and 7 per cent of the urban labour force), the male participation rate would have been about 65 per cent if all 10-year-olds and above were included. In fact it is no greater than 57 per cent, indicating, perhaps, the low proportion of children included. On the other hand, the peculiar definition of 'immoral occupation' and the exclusion of property owners would appear to create a downward bias.

2.3 IMPLICATIONS OF DEMOGRAPHIC FACTORS FOR
THE DEVELOPMENT PATTERN

Bangladesh has a population density of 1306 per square mile
(1970/71) which is the highest for all countries of any reasonable
size in the whole world. The nearest comparisons are to be
found in the Netherlands (1065 in 1969), Taiwan (1039 in
1968), Belgium (890 in 1969) and Japan (770 in 1969).[1] The
full implication of such density of population cannot, however,
be understood from such a comparison. To begin to understand
the true magnitude of the problem, it must be realised that 75
per cent of the population depend directly on the land for their
living. For every person depending almost exclusively on land
as a source of income (i.e. for each member of the farming
families) the available cultivable acreage is only 0·445 on the
average. The average family size being 5·65,[2] this means that
an average family of nearly six persons have to eke out a living
from a farm of 2·5 acres only.

The gravity of the demographic situation is more startlingly
revealed when the annual increments are considered. No one is
absolutely certain about the various demographic parameters,
but the PGE Survey provides reasonably reliable estimates.
The crude birthrate is believed to have been at the peak of 54·9
per thousand in the mid-sixties. It is believed to have come down
slightly by 1970, perhaps to about 50 per thousand. Crude death
rate has been 19·6 per thousand.[3] The country may well have
briefiy experienced a more than 3 per cent growth rate in the
recent past and, once the society settles down after the recent
turmoil, it is unlikely to have a population growth rate significantly less than 3 per cent in the near future (assuming, of
course, no more than a conventional success of the family
planning programme).

[1] Apart from the small pockets like the Holy See, East and West Berlin,
Monaco, Barbados, Bermuda, Spanish North Africa and Macau, the
United Nations Statistical Yearbook (1969) lists only two territories with a
population of more than one million which have greater population density:
Hong Kong (10,547 per square mile with a total of 3·9 million in 1968) and
Singapore (9506 per square mile with a total of 2 million).
[2] East Pakistan Bureau of Statistics, *Master Survey of Agriculture Seventh
Round – Phase I, 1968* (mimeographed).
[3] Bean, L. L. *et al.*, op. cit.

In the immediate future, these demographic rates would lead to an annual addition of just over two million to the population of Bangladesh. To get a feeling of the order of magnitude involved, it may suffice to say that in less than two years the *increment* to population alone would amount to the size of the existing population of Norway. The magnitude of the burden can be conveyed through a few numerical illustrations. If we assume that a unit of income can be generated through the addition of two and a quarter units of capital assests at the margin (i.e. the incremental capital-output ratio is 2·25) and that replacement of capital is a modest 3 per cent of current output, then nearly ten per cent of GDP will have to be saved and invested merely to provide for the population the dismally low present standard of living.

Again, assuming that the participation rate at the margin is no greater than average, the annual addition to the labour force will be as high as 0·75 million. Given the already existing massive unemployment and underemployment in the economy, no planner would want to set an additional employment target below this number. Also, considering the very low land/man ratio, it would be natural to try to create this amount of employment outside agriculture. Observed capital-labour ratios in the large and medium-scale manufacturing industries and in the economic infrastructure have been very high in the past. This was partly because of the more than socially desirable capital-intensity of blueprints and partly because of excess capacity,[1] but much of it is in the nature of these sectors. Jute and cotton textiles seem to have roughly the median capital-intensities. If these industries were run at full capacity, their average capital-intensity in the mid-sixties could perhaps have been brought down to Rs. 8500 per person. Making a further heroic assumption that by a combination of policies aimed at saving capital this ratio could be reduced to Rs. 6000, the investment requirement for the fulfilment of the minimum employment target by conventional means of industrialisation (carried out with rare efficiency) would be Rs. 4500 million. This is about 50 per cent higher than the average annual

---

[1] Khan, A. R., 'Capital-Intensity and The Efficiency of Factor Use', *The Pakistan Development Review*. Autumn 1970.

Population and Standard of Living

investment level in Bangladesh during 1965–70 and would be around 18 per cent of its current GDP.[1]

TABLE 2.1

DEMOGRAPHIC FEATURES OF BANGLADESH

	1960/61	1963/64	1966/67	1970/71
Population				
(million)	53·4	58·8	64·6	72·0
Urban	2·8	3·3	3·9	4·7
Rural	50·6	55·5	60·7	67·3
Population				
Growth Rate				
(%)		3·25	3·15	2·75
Population				
Density				
(per sq. mile)	—	—	—	1,306
Land/Man				
Ratio in				
Agriculture				
(acre/				
person)	—	—	—	0·445
Labour Force				
(million)	—	—	22·29	24·84
Urban	—	—	1·38	1·66
Rural	—	—	20·91	23·18

NOTES

1960/61 population is from Bean *et al.*, op. cit., which was arrived at by age and sex specific adjustments in the 1961 Census estimates on the basis of PGE and other information. This shows a 5 per cent undernumeration in the 1961 Census (giving mid-1960/61 population).

The method of estimating 1970/71 population has been shown in the text. For 1963/64 and 1966/67, estimates have been arrived at from the nearest period estimates in Bean *et al.*, op. cit. by using their growth rates.

Urban population for 1960/61 is estimated by using the 1961 urbanisation ratio of 5·19 per cent. For later years, the elasticity of urbanisation with respect to total population is assumed to be 1·73. Land/man ratio shows the amount of land per person for those dependent on agriculture as a means of living.

[1] These number are approximate. The 1965–70 investment figures at current prices are from the then Government of East Pakistan publication *East Pakistan Economic Survey, 1969–70.* GDP estimates should be at early sixties prices which are used for capital-intensity measures. At 1959–60 prices, the GDP of Bangladesh for 1969–70 was estimated by the CSO to be just over 20·22 thousand million.

What the above-illustrations serve to demonstrate is that it is impossible to be optimistic about the economic prospects of Bangladesh as long as one is confined to the conventional ideas of demographic transition and industrial development.

In the recent past, the country witnessed some effort at reducing the birthrate through popularising family planning. The programme consisted almost exclusively of subsidising the various contraceptive means and publicising the virtues of smaller families. Coming from an authoritarian government which was identified with the policies which increased the impoverishment of the masses and accelerated the inequality of income distribution, such exhortations rarely rang true. More important, the programme did not incorporate essential social reforms on marriage, divorce, women's status, etc., and completely side-tracked the educational and cultural prerequisites. In the Western world, demographic transition was preceded by industrialisation, higher living standards, universal education and complete social and cultural transformation. Such transition took place over a long period. If in Bangladesh such a transition is to be brought about quickly before industrialisation and high living standards, it is too much to hope that this can be achieved even without the necessary social reform.

It is not surprising that population planning in the past has been so unambitious. Such a programme had the objective of reducing the birthrate only modestly; a projection of the Bangladesh population of 83 million by 1975 was cited as a would-be example of the result of a very successful family planning programme.[1] It is important to realise that even a complete 'success' of such an impotent programme would leave the growing population a crippling burden on the economy of Bangladesh.

As we do not intend to return to this very important problem in the later parts, we might briefly sketch the requirement of public policy. Since the objective is to have an unconventional demographic transition and since nothing but an unprecedented (even by Japanese standards) transformation will ease the burden, reliance must be placed on unconventional means. The political leadership must give due priority to an ambitious

[1] See Bean *et al.*, op. cit., section VII.

family planning programme. Coming from a popular, representative government, the programme should have greater credibility. This should be buttressed by overall economic policy of better distribution so that the connection between fewer children and a higher standard of living becomes quickly established. Also necessary reforms regarding marriage and divorce laws, status of women, minimum social security and related areas must be enacted and implemented. The objective must be to reduce the birthrate to half its present level not in twenty-five to fifty years but in five to ten years. This cannot even be approached through conventional bureaucratic channels.

The other aspect of the problem, that of deciding how to deploy the vast manpower and its increment, must also be solved in a way unconventional to the eyes of those who simplify the economic progress of the backward world as being merely the process of industrialisation through the adoption of the available technology in the industrial economies and its substitution for traditional activities. The poverty is so dismal and the labour force so vast that it will simply be impossible to generate enough internal savings to equip merely the incremental labour force with modern technology. Efforts must constantly be made to adopt such technology selectively and complementarily with those of the traditional ones which prove efficient in the context of a given relative resource endowment. But at the same time, the possible bi-modal income distribution due to the co-existence of modern and traditional techniques must be avoided. Sensible planning must recognise the vital role of demographic reality in shaping the economic system of Bangladesh.

3 Past Growth and Present Standard of Living

3.1 GROWTH AND STAGNATION OVER THE LAST TWO DECADES

At the time Bangladesh was partitioned out of India as the eastern wing of Pakistan, it had little modern industry. During the quarter-century of its partnership with Pakistan, Bangladesh had a mild rate of modern industrialisation with little overall growth. Also the traditional small-scale industries achieved very little growth and some actually declined.

The conventional way of measuring growth and structural change is to look at the changes in the level and composition of domestic product. In Table 3.1 such information has been put together for a number of years over the last two decades.

Accepting for the moment the GDP series as a reasonable approximation of changes in real output, the first thing we note is that income per head grew at an annual exponential rate of only 0·27 per cent.[1] From the information over the two decades, it is best to conclude that the long-term rate of growth in *per capita* income has not been significantly different from zero.

The GDP estimates are, however, well known to be based on highly unsatisfactory practices. Value added in a number of sectors is assumed to grow at a constant annual rate, arbitrarily assumed as equal to or higher than the rate of population growth.[2] These sectors are fishery, most of livestock production, small-scale industries, housing and services. Together they have been about a quarter of GDP in recent years. Thus the methodology of the GDP estimates have a built-in protection against *per capita* decline (in fact for modest *per capita* increase) of a quarter of GDP. It is important to note, however, that these are, by all

[1] That is ·0027 is the value of b in the regression equation $\log y = a + bt$ where y = income per head, t = time (0 for 49/50, 5 for 54/55 etc.).

[2] See the methodology outlined in the CSO, *The Final Report of the National Income Commission.*

available evidence, the lagging sectors. The assumption that
their outputs *per capita* have even been maintained would appear
to be biased upwards. Thus the comparison between the housing
censuses in 1950 and 1960 shows that the annual growth rate
has been well below 1 per cent per year.[1] Similarly, cottage
industries have been growing at less than 2 per cent per year
since 1960.[2] A comparison of 1961 National Sample Survey with
the Quarterly Surveys of Current Economic Condition of 1963/
1964 and 1966/67 shows that the consumption per head of fish
has been declining rather drastically.[3]

If the assumption of steady trend increase of the aforemen-
tioned one-quarter of GDP is abandoned and a more realistic
rate from available indicators substituted, the GDP *per capita*
will almost certainly show a decline over the two decades.

These, of course, are not the only sources of overstatement in
the rate of growth. There have been new methods of estimation
incorporated with the passage of time which have not been
extended to past years. These methodological changes have
nearly always meant an improved coverage. Even the method of
crop output estimation has 'improved' in the sense of increasing
the ratio of reported production to the alternative estimate of
consumption from family budget surveys (see below). It does
not appear to be an accidental or 'random' error that during the
sixties, the decade during which nationalism in Bangladesh
became increasingly militant and the central Pakistan Government went all out to prove that efforts were being made to
channel more resources into what was then its eastern wing,
almost every component seems to have suffered from such systematic overstatement. Even large-scale manufacturing, which is
supposed to have a reliable basis of information, is not exempt.
Thus the Censuses of Manufacturing Industries (CMI) show that
value added in large-scale industries at *current prices* went up by
50·2 per cent between 1962/63 and 1967/68.[4] If allowance is

[1] Housing census quoted in CSO, *Statistical Pocketbook of Pakistan*, 1963.
[2] East Pakistan Small Industries Corporation, *Survey of Cottage Industries in East Pakistan*.
[3] CSO, *Statistical Yearbook 1968*, Table 206. The 1966/67 Quarterly
Survey is unpublished but the results were made available by the CSO.
[4] See CSO, *Census of Manufacturing Industries 1962–63 to 1965–66. Summary
Statistics*, and East Pakistan Bureau of Statistics, *Census of Manufacturing
Industries in East Pakistan 1967–68* (both mimeographed).

TABLE 3.1

GROWTH AND STRUCTURAL CHANGE IN BANGLADESH 1949/50 TO 1969/70

(values at constant 1959/60 prices)

Year	GDP (million Rs.)	GDP per capita (Rs.)	Sectoral Shares of GDP (%)				
			Agriculture	Large-scale Industry	Small-scale Industry	Construction Transport Power	Services
1949/50	12,374	293	65·2	0·6	3·3	5·6	25·3
1954/55	13,816	290	63·0	1·4	3·3	6·6	25·7
1960/61	15,310	287	62·6	3·0	3·4	7·5	23·5
1963/64	17,855	304	59·4	3·4	3·1	11·3	22·8
1966/67	18,734	290	55·9	5·0	3·2	12·2	23·7
1969/70	22,317	316	55·3	6·0	2·9	12·8	23·0

NOTE

GDP for 1949/50 and 1954/55 from Khan, T. M. and A. Bergan 'Measurement of Structural Change in the Pakistan Economy', *The Pakistan Development Review*, summer 1966; GDP for 1960/61 onwards from *East Pakistan Economic Survey 1969/70*. Both are based on the official Planning Commission revision of the CSO estimates. Population for 1949/50 and 1954/55 from Khan and Bergan, op. cit., which are Planning Commission estimates. The value of the coefficient b is ·0027 in the equation log $y = a + bt$ where $y =$ GDP per capita, t is time (0 for year 1949/50, 5 for year 1954/55, 20 for year 1969/70). The Planning Commission population series would make population estimates in more recent years relatively higher. If these were used, the value of b would have been less.

made for price increase and the likely improvement in coverage over time, the real growth rate would perhaps be no more than around 33 per cent.[1] But the GDP accounts show a growth rate for this component of 84 per cent over the same period. No justification is provided for this, although one suspects that in practice only one benchmark CMI has been used and for the subsequent years an inflated and unpublished industrial production index has been applied.[2]

There seems to be little doubt that the average standard of living in the sense of *per capita* GDP at constant prices was at best stagnant over the two decades; indeed it is more likely to have declined. In view of the generally shaky statistical basis of GDP estimates, it would be desirable to look for alternative indicators of change in standard of living. In Table 3.2 we assemble indices of real wages of urban and rural workers. It can easily be seen that for both industrial and rural wages there is no upward trend to be discerned. In view of the near certainty that the relevant cost of living indices are understated, it is probable that the real wage rates actually declined steadily.[3] What the intertemporal trend of real wages shows is that the standard of living of the lowest of the income groups, the rural poor, deteriorated relatively to the average. If one assumes that over the long period income per head for the whole population remained constant, then this would also apply to the industrial workers.[4] Given the easily observed but so far unquantified phenomenon of an appreciable rise in the living standards of the upper income groups in the urban areas, it would be reasonable to conclude that the stagnation in the average standard of living was accompanied by increasing inequality of income distribution.

[1] Price increase for manufactures was 12·7 per cent over the same period according to the CSO, *Statistical Year book 1968*.

[2] This presumption is based on the author's impression during his brief participation in the so-called experts' group of the National Accounts Committee during 1970.

[3] See the references to the papers originally containing the indices, at the bottom of Table 3·2, for arguments.

[4] As discussed in the original paper, the insignificant rise in the overall industrial wage index is almost certainly due to a change in the composition of industries; wage rates in large, homogeneous industries like jute textiles are more accurate indicators.

TABLE 3.2

REAL WAGES OF URBAN AND RURAL WORKERS

Year	Wages in Urban Industries Index			Rural Wages Year	Index
	All Industries	Jute Textiles	Cotton Textiles		
1954	100·0		100·0	1949	100·0
				1950	94·8
1955	88·4	103·2		1951	77·7
1957	91·4	84·9		1955	92·8
1958	93·6	88·5		1959	88·5
				1960	88·0
1959/60	92·8		94·6	1961	100·5
			101·8		
1962/63	96·4			1965	96·9
1967/68	101·1	94·6	81·7	1966	82·3

SOURCE
Industrial wages from A. R. Khan, 'What Has Been Happening to Real Wages in Pakistan?', *The Pakistan Development Review*, autumn 1967, and commentary to Part IV of Keith Griffin and A. R. Khan, *Growth and Inequality in Pakistan* (Macmillan, 1972). Rural wages from S. R. Bose, 'Trend of Real Income of the Rural Poor,' *The Pakistan Development Review*, autumn 1968.

Further evidence of the movement in the standard of living would be the change in *per capita* consumption of the major consumption goods, if such information were available. The most important of such goods would be rice which, for much of the period, was nearly 40 per cent of the market value of the total national consumption and about 35 per cent of GDP. It would be unthinkable that the average living standard could rise without an increase in *per capita* consumption of rice unless, of course, income distribution takes a very sharp unfavourable turn. This is because at the present level of average consumption, the income elasticity of demand for rice has been found to be rather high. As Table 3.3 indicates, on the evidence of both family budget data and aggregate availability data, rice consumption *per capita* declined. To a certain extent, this was made up by the increased consumption of what is considered an inferior substitute, wheat, but even the aggregate consumption of cereals shows a slight downward, rather than any upward, trend.

It would therefore appear beyond all reasonable doubt that the average standard of living in Bangladesh showed no upward trend over the two decades of her partnership with Pakistan. Income distribution almost certainly became less equitable and as a result the vast majority of the population, the urban and the rural poor, experienced a steady decline in their standard of living.

One final point about the rate of growth may be made. The GDP estimates, as well as the other estimates of real value of income and consumption, are all based on domestic market prices. As we shall see, these market prices had no correspondence to social scarcities or even market scarcities as reflected in world trade. The domestic market prices relative to the scarcity prices were made higher through excessive protection for the fast-growing sectors. Thus the social rate of growth that one might estimate by substituting the market prices by social scarcity indices would be lower than the rate of growth shown by GDP estimates.[1]

TABLE 3·3

PER CAPITA CONSUMPTION OF RICE AND WHEAT

(lbs/person/day)

	From Budget Survey Data		From Aggregate Availability Data	
	Rice	Rice and Wheat	Rice	Rice and Wheat
1960/61	—	—	1·04	1·07
1961	1·11	1·12	—	—
1963/64	0·94	1·01	1·02	1·09
1966/67	—	—	0·85	0·91
1968/69	—	—	0·92	1·01
1969/70	—	—	0·96	1·06

SOURCE
1961 Budget Survey figure from National Sample Survey Third Round, the 1963/64 from the Quarterly Survey of Current Economic Conditions, both quoted in the CSO *Statistical Yearbook 1968*. The availability figure, from *East Pakistan Economic Survey 1969/70*, shows net production plus import divided by population.

The stagnation in *per capita* income was accompanied by some mild industrialisation raising the contribution of large-scale

[1] The calculations have been made using the estimates of the accounting prices developed in Chapter 10. The social rate of growth is indeed found to be smaller than that shown by GDP estimates at market prices.

industries[1] from nearly nothing in 1949/50 to about 6 per cent of GDP by 1969/70. We have argued above that on the basis of the information in the available censuses of manufacturing, even this would appear to have been overestimated. Even if one were to take the estimates as accurate, there would be no reason to call it a very fast rate of industrialisation. According to the latest CMI (1967/68) only about 1·02 per cent of the nation's labour force are employed in the large- and medium-scale industries. Industrialisation in the sense of a decreasing share of agriculture in total labour force could clearly not have occurred with this rate of industrial employment in recent years. In fact agriculture's share of labour force is known to have increased from 84·7 per cent in 1951 to 85·3 per cent in 1961 as shown by the two population censuses. What has happened to the share in more recent years is not known with any confidence. The 1966/67 estimate of 77·8 per cent, on the basis of a Labour Force Sample Survey,[2] is almost certainly influenced by the difference in definitions and methodology from the previous population censuses as well as the possibly high sampling error. In view of the fact that the percentage share of large-scale industries has increased from 0·8 per cent to only 1·02 per cent and the evidence that small scale industries have been growing at a rate slower than that of population, it is doubtful whether agriculture's share has shown any significant decline.

A few brief points, to be discussed later at much greater length, may be made about the nature of industrialisation. Even according to the GDP accounts, the share of small-scale industries has been declining. Independent and direct sources of data reveal an even lower rate of growth.[3] It is well known that much of indigenous skill has been allowed to die out. An outstanding example is small-scale hosiery in which there

---

[1] The definition of large-scale industry is itself a bit tricky. The CMI covers the 2(j) factories (those employing 20 or more workers and using power) and, for some recent years, 5(1) factories (employing 10 or more with or without power). Thus large-scale seems to be an inappropriate name. They are characterised by modern technology and include both large- and medium-scale enterprises. It appears that there would be considerable overlap between large-scale and small-scale as shown in the GDP accounts since its large-scale refers to the CMI industries.

[2] CSO, *Population and Labour Force July 1966–June 1967*.

[3] East Pakistan Small Industries Corporation, op. cit.

existed a good deal of traditional skill which has not survived. Also the growth of weaving, the largest cottage enterprise, has lagged. No detailed information is available about the causes of their decline, but from rudimentary knowledge it would appear that they were systematically starved of raw materials (particularly yarn) while nothing was done to help them face the much more powerful marketing organisation of large-scale producers, often in West Pakistan, trading behind the shelter of high effective protection.

The modern industries were set up through a great many incentives which will be discussed more fully later. Their profit was ensured at a high rate through massive protection. They were provided with underpriced foreign exchange to import capital and intermediate goods and cheap credit from the oligopolistic banks owned by the industrialists themselves. Depreciation allowances were high, as much as 40 per cent in the first year for machinery and equipment. Taxes were low and tax laws allowed much of the consumption of the capitalists and top management to be charged as business costs. Trade union-ism was brutally suppressed.

To be sure, these incentives were not provided for the indus-trialisation of Bangladesh. For a quarter-century Bangladesh had complete economic union with West Pakistan. It is the development of West Pakistani capitalists that the above incen-tives were mainly aimed at. Industrialisation mainly took place in West Pakistan. The distribution of import licences, the direct control of investment allocation and the numerous other policy instruments ensured that. The little industrialisation that Bangladesh had could be explained in the following way: (*a*) there were industries whose location in Bangladesh was war-ranted by the availability of raw materials (e.g. jute and paper). These were developed either directly under West Pakistani ownership or under public sector ownership, to be transferred later to the private capitalists in West Pakistan. Thus a very high proportion of Bangladesh manufacturing was owned by West Pakistani capitalists. (*b*) There were marginal cases of Bengali capitalists who also benefited from the system. This group increased its share in later years with the emergence of Bengali nationalism as a political force confronting the central Pakistan Government. But they were both individually and collectively the smaller partners of the West Pakistani capitalists.

To summarise, Bangladesh, during her two and a half decades of union in Pakistan, had no significant increase in income per head. The standard of living for the vast majority in the lower income brackets almost certainly declined. There was some, though by no means dramatic, progress in modern industrialisation, largely under foreign West Pakistani ownership and through the wasteful use of capital and capital-intensive techniques. Such industrialisation was promoted by massive incentives provided by the government. The traditional small-scale and cottage industries declined through deliberate neglect and negative policies.

3.2 THE QUANTIFICATION OF POVERTY

When we describe the current standard of living as *per capita* income of Rs. 316 at 1959/60 prices or probably about Rs. 450 at today's prices,[1] what kind of picture is implied? At the latest reported exchange rate,[2] this would be just under 7 new British pence or about 17 US cents per person per day. A more striking description is the living standard of the poorest 20 per cent. From Ashjorn Bergan's study we know that the poorest 20 per cent of Bengalees receive 7 per cent of the GDP.[3] Thus the *average* annual income per head of the poorest 20 per cent would be Rs. 157·5 or just under 2½ new pence or 6 US cents per person per day.

Extreme though the poverty of Bangladesh is, such quantification is apt to bewilder people in the outside world for the simple fact that the equivalent incomes just mentioned would certainly mean rapid starvation in the Western world. And we know that in spite of a good deal of death through slow starvation, people in Bangladesh on the average not only manage to

[1] Index of wholesale prices for 1969/70 according to the CSO was 146 (1959/60 being 100). The GDP deflator for the whole of Pakistan in that year was 136 approximately.

[2] According to reports in January, the Bangladesh rupee (named 'Taka') has been devalued from the old Pakistan rate, to the rate of the Indian rupee, making £1 = Rs. 18·9 approximately.

[3] 'Personal Income Distribution and Personal Saving 1963/64', *The Pakistan Development Review*, summer 1967.

live two score and odd years, if not the biblical three score and ten, but also to achieve a 3 per cent annual growth.

We shall, therefore, try to give a detailed account of real consumption per head, as well as some idea of the variation of such consumption between income groups, in order to represent concretely the existing standard of living. To begin with, it should be remembered that even when the values of housing and self-produced consumption are imputed, about 73 per cent of the consumption of the rural population (who constitute over 93 per cent of the nation's population) consists of food. Even for the urban areas, food accounts for more than 62 per cent of total consumption.[1] Much of the remainder is accounted for by housing (14 per cent in rural and 18 per cent in urban areas) and clothing and footwear (5 per cent in rural and 6 per cent in urban areas). Thus by describing the consumption of food alone, we can account for nearly three-quarters of the living standard.

The most comprehensive account of food consumption is available from the nutrition survey of 1962–4.[2] This is somewhat old, but as we have seen above, it is more likely that average consumption of important grains and average standard of living have gone down rather than up since that date.

Compared to the contemporary family budget surveys, the consumption figures for rice seem to be high, particularly for rural areas. While the nutrition survey is likely to be more accurate in measurement since actual weighing was carried out, it is likely that it was more subject to seasonality as a single day's observation was noted. We should be safe in accepting these figures as upper limits of current food consumption.

Table 3.4 summarises some useful information about food intake. It is seen that, on the average, calorie in rural areas and vitamin C in both areas are the only requirements fulfilled; a significant deficiency exists in calorie intake in urban areas, and in protein and nearly all other vitamins in both urban and rural areas. Part C of the table is perhaps even more illuminating. It shows that although the average calorie intake is adequate in

[1] CSO, *Statistical Yearbook 1968*, shows the results of the family expenditure survey 1966/67.

[2] U.S. Department of Health, Education and Welfare, *Nutrition Survey of East Pakistan, March 1962–January 1964*, May 1966.

rural areas, more than 45 per cent of the families are below the acceptable level.

Similarly, two-thirds to four-fifths of the families are deficient in protein and vitamins. To summarise, food intake is not only qualitatively inadequate on the average, but also quantitatively below starvation level for nearly half the population. It is extremely deficient in 'protective' elements.

From food let us move on to clothing. We find that in 1966/67 annual *per capita* consumption was $7\frac{1}{2}$ yards of average quality long cloth equivalent in rural areas and $12\frac{1}{2}$ yards in urban areas.[1] This would barely work out at one set of clothing per person in rural areas during a twelve-month period. Perhaps for a vast proportion of the population there is no more than a couple of loin cloths per year.

Little information is available for rural housing except that out of gross expenditure on housing a very high proportion, according to the family expenditure surveys, consists of repair and maintenance. A hut that has to be replaced completely every two to three years can hardly be called building capital and it requires imaginative accountants to quantify its imputed rental for inclusion as housing service.[2] A vast majority of these dwellings literally offer no protection against nature. For urban housing, we have better information. An analysis of a sample of about 1100 such dwellings in the three largest urban industrial centres shows that an average family of 5·6 members have on the average 1·5 rooms. Nearly 71 per cent are temporary constructions without any masonry, 56 per cent have only one room, 82 per cent have no water connection and 97 per cent have no electricity.[3]

The above should enable the reader to imagine the dismally low level of consumption of goods and services by the 'average' people of Bangladesh. It should also be clear that nearly half the population are on a starvation diet, nearly 90 per cent have

[1] These are found by dividing the expenditure on clothing, footwear, linen and bedding by the price per yard of average quality long cloth. The former is obtained from the CSOs unpublished *Quarterly Survey of Current Economic Conditions 1966/67*. The latter is from the CSO *Statistical Yearbook 1968*.

[2] Note that as a result, all repair and maintenance expenditures, which should be treated as current inputs, is included in GDP.

[3] CSO, *Statistical Yearbook 1968*.

TABLE 3.4
FOOD CONSUMPTION

A

	Rural	Urban
Rice	1·111	0·687
Other cereals	0·070	0·113
Starchy roots	0·122	0·070
Sugar and sweets	0·016	0·026
Pulses and nuts	0·062	0·058
Vegetables	0·296	0·296
Fruit	0·022	0·039
Meat	0·013	0·043
Eggs	0·004	0·006
Fish	0·072	0·092
Milk and Cheese	0·038	0·117
Fats and oils	0·014	0·030
Miscellaneous spices	0·010	0·022

B

Per capita nutrient intake

	Rural		Urban	
	Observed	Reco'd	Observed	Rec'd
Calories	2251	2150	1732	2130
Protein (gm)	57·5	61·5	49·5	61·7
Fat (gm)	17·7	—	25·0	—
Carbohydrates (gm)	476·0	—	327·0	—
Calcium (mg)	304·0	494·0	226	482
Iron (mg)	9·7	12·1	8·5	12·2
Vitamin A (IU)	1590	3057	1795	3036
Thiamine (mg)	1·47	0·86	1·03	0·85
Riboflavin (mg)	0·53	0·86	0·54	0·85
Niacin (mg)	22·8	14·2	14·3	14·1
Vitamin C (mg)	39·6	28·5	38·5	28·8

C

Percentage of Households with nutrient intakes below acceptable level

	Rural	Urban
Calories	45·7	76·4
Protein	60·8	77·2
Calcium	85·8	93·9
Iron	67·9	79·6
Vitamin A	83·8	80·8
Thiamine	15·5	39·1
Riboflavin	86·6	80·3
Niacin	7·8	37·9
Vitamin C	60·1	59·3

NOTE

Food intake was actually weighed for a 24-hour period and samples taken to determine nutrient. Acceptable levels are based on FAO requirement for given height, weight, age, sex and environmental temperature. Rural sample covered 10,599 persons in 17 rural locations spread over 17 districts. Urban sample covered 4137 persons in five urban centres.

some kind of deficiency in food, and that a vast majority are ill-clad and nearly shelterless.

The effect of such poor living conditions is the low expectation of life – 49·2 years for men and 46·9 years for women at birth – as compared to over 70 years in the western countries. Infant mortality rate is 153 for male and 128 for female per thousand, as compared to less than 20 in the developed nations.[1]

Illiteracy is widespread. According to the 1961 census only 17·6 per cent were literate in the sense of being able to 'read a short statement on everyday life in any language'. The fact that the 1968 Master Survey of Agriculture finds the rural literacy rate as high as 25·7 per cent is certainly at least partly due to the use of a lower standard in measuring literacy. All available indicators suggest that literacy over the last decade has progressed extremely slowly.

3.3 IMPLICATIONS FOR PLANNING OBJECTIVES

In the context of the above, it is no longer in doubt what the priorities of sensible planning must be. It no longer makes sense to talk merely in terms of rates of growth when so much depends on how the increment is distributed. A social sense of priority would require the concentration of effort in the immediate future on bringing the calorie starved 45 per cent above the starvation line. Closely following this must be the objective of raising the overall quality of food and the provision of housing and clothing, with greater emphasis on the needs of those whose consumption is below the average. Health and mass literacy should next be emphasised.

Mere emphasis on the overall growth rate will not necessarily solve these problems. In fact the last two decades of development planning in the then Pakistan is an outstanding example of emphasising the objective of overall growth. It was argued that the preoccupation with the problem of income distribution would slow down the rate of growth as it would call for distributing income away from the 'saving class', i.e. the capitalists, and in favour of the non-saving poorer classes. In the name of promoting growth, income was redistributed in favour of the (West

[1] These demographic characteristics have been taken from Bean *et al.*, op. cit.

Pakistani) capitalists and traders through exchange rate policy and fiscal policy, through the distribution at nominal prices of the entitlement to scarce resources, through the suppression of working-class organisations and a host of other direct and indirect measures. As a result, there has been 'impressive industrialisation' in West Pakistan. But income distribution became worse, aggravating many of the above problems. What is more, the 'saving classes' do not seem to have saved at anything near the expected rate; their saving, by all indication, has been considerably lower than the estimated transfer of income to them from the poorer social classes through the direct controls on exchange rate and the rationing of the import entitlements alone. Moreover, what appears to be 'impressive industrialisation', giving the industrialists enormous control over resources, is on closer scrutiny of much lower value to the society when its contribution to real income is accounted for by evaluating all inputs and outputs in relation to true social scarcities rather than at distorted prices resulting from high and non-uniform effective protection.[1] If the balance of political power at the central government had been different, Bangladesh could have had a share of such industrialisation and growth while the problem of poverty would have remained unsolved and just as pressing! If there is anything that Bangladesh should learn from its association with Pakistan, it is the senselessness of the planning strategy pursued therein.

3.4 THE CAUSE OF PAST STAGNATION: A BRIEF COMMENT

Although we do not intend to enter into a full discussion of the problems, we would briefly analyse the main cause of the past stagnation and give a short account of the alleged resource transfer out of Bangladesh in the past. The stagnation in Bangladesh is primarily explained by the low rate of investment, including a low rate of public sector investment. Because of its political union with West Pakistan and complete domination by the latter in the authoritarian Central Government which had the monopoly of economic power, Bangladesh naturally

[1] For an analysis of the strategy see Griffin, Keith, and A. R. Khan (eds), *Growth and Inequality in Pakistan* (Macmillan, 1972)

had a low priority in public investment. Largely because of the lack of government patronage and the lack of access to the entitlements to the scarce resources controlled and distributed by the government, the private capitalists (*vis-à-vis* their counterparts in the West) remained weak and ineffective and were unable to achieve a high rate of private investment. In the agricultural sector, the low rates of investment and saving were explained by, apart from the general poverty of peasant agriculture in a situation of low land/man ratio and backward technology, the massive concealed taxation of and disincentives to agriculture. The overall rate of gross investment in the Bangladesh economy even in fairly recent years has been no more than 11 per cent of GDP.[1]

There is, however, no reason to think that the society was not being subjected to the pressures of a high rate of accumulation. In fact the population of Bangladesh, particularly the 90-odd per cent who constitute the rural population, were subjected to a high rate of 'primitive capital accumulation' which was transferred to finance the growth of West Pakistani capitalism and industrialisation.

A complete understanding of the mechanism of such transfer will never be clear without detailed flow-of-funds accounts between Bangladesh and West Pakistan during the quarter-century of their political association, and for understandable reasons such accounts have been kept a closely-guarded secret by the State Bank of Pakistan. But some understanding of the mechanism is possible from the information about trade flows and the operation of the system of direct controls on trade.

In the earlier years, some resource transfer must have been financed through the central government balance of revenues and expenditure. Less than a quarter of central government expenditure was located in Bangladesh while a much higher proportion of its revenue originated there. Again, actual quantification is impossible owing to the secrecy surrounding the relevant regional statistics, although the general direction

[1] This is the ratio of aggregate private and public development expenditure during 1966–70 to GDP during the same period, both converted into current price estimates. Note that 'development expenditure' contains some amount of non-investment outlay.

should be beyond all reasonable doubt to anyone familiar with the orders of magnitude involved.

A much more sophisticated and quantitatively important mechanism was instituted through the policies regarding the control of foreign trade, whose basic elements can be described as follows. The domestic currency (rupee) was kept artificially overvalued by a big margin. Imports were subjected to direct quantitative restrictions. Entitlements to import were rationed among chosen recipients. Exporters were compelled to surrender their foreign exchange earnings at the artificially low rupee price and import entitlements were sold to the chosen traders at this low price.

Through the first decade and a half of Pakistan, Bangladesh had a huge surplus in trade with the outside world. It was made to give up its surplus foreign exchange at an artificially low price. The West Pakistani traders were given import entitlement against this foreign exchange which they used to import goods and earn massive profits in the starved domestic market, often in Bangladesh itself. The effect was of concealed taxation on the export surplus region (Bangladesh) and the producers of exportables (principally the poor growers of jute) and a corresponding concealed subsidy to the traders receiving the import entitlements (mostly the West Pakistani traders and capitalists). The high profit on the sale of imports provided these capitalists with much of their original capital. Again, it was with the use of such profit earned in the Bangladesh market, rather than through the classical way of undergoing an initial period of capital exports, that West Pakistani capitalists came to own the means of production in Bangladesh. This ownership, extending over much of the modern industries, tea plantations and trade, later facilitated both a net transfer of profit and the internal growth of such ownership.

It is useful to divide the transfer of resources into three components: (i) the value of goods and services exported abroad by Bangladesh less the value of the goods and services imported from abroad, the balance adjusted for the overvaluation of the exchange rate, $P(X-M)$ where P = ratio of 'true' to official price of foreign exchange in terms of rupees; (ii) the balance of regional trade $(X^r - M^r)$; and (iii) the share of Bangladesh in total foreign aid inflow, adjusted for the overvaluation of foreign exchange, αPA, where α = share of Bangladesh and A = total capital inflow in the then Pakistan. Thus, total outflow of resources from Bangladesh would amount to

$$P(X-M) + (X^r - M^r) + \alpha PA$$

In order to arrive at a quantitative measurement it would be necessary to establish the values of P and α. In spite of considerable dispute about the actual value, all available studies indicate that $P = 1\cdot67$ (i.e. foreign exchange had a true value of two-thirds more in terms of rupees) is something like a lower limit. A value of α would be even more difficult to establish. But a lower limit seems to be implied by the proportion of the value of the aid projects actually approved for location in Bangladesh. This would suggest a value between $0\cdot2$ and $0\cdot3$ for α. Another possibility is to equate α with the share of Bangladesh in the total population of the then Pakistan, which was about $0\cdot55$.

It is important to note that for about a decade and a half after the birth of Pakistan, the following relation held for Bangladesh:

$$(X-M) + (X^r - M^r) > O$$

so that irrespective of the values of α and P, there was an unambiguous transfer of resources. Since the early sixties $(X-M)$ has had slightly positive or slightly negative values and the sum of $(X-M)$ and $(X^r - M^r)$ has been negative. Thus, an estimate of resource transfer for these years will have to be based on plausible values of P and α. Using $P = 1\cdot67$, Bangladesh can be shown to have made a substantial resource transfer even if the value of α is as low as $0\cdot2$. Thus, for example, during the three recent years, 1966/67 to 1968/69, $P(X-M) + (X^r - M^r)$ has been much less than $0\cdot2\ PA$ in absolute value.

For a plausible quantification of the resource transfer over the two decades leading to 1968/69, one could refer to the figure of Rs. 31,120 million arrived at by a group of highly competent economists on the basis of a detailed analysis.[1] The annual average of this is about 10 per cent of the current-price

---

[1] Government of Pakistan, Planning Commission, *Report of the Panel of Economists on the Fourth Five-Year Plan*, May 1970, p. 75. The estimate is the one contained in the report of the East Pakistan members and is based on the assumption that $\alpha = \cdot55$.

GDP of the median year. Even if foreign assistance is left out of consideration, Bangladesh would appear to have been subjected to a substantial rate of resource transfer.

A point to note about the concealed taxation through the exchange rate policy is that its burden was borne by the poorer sections of the population, the growers of jute. Jute is not grown in plantations. Even a small peasant would produce a bit to satisfy his cash requirements. In Bangladesh few farms could be called large by any standard. The growers of jute could not have been any better off than the average farmers. Taking a typical year, 1959/60, and assuming a modest value of $P = 1.67$, the concealed taxation on the growers of jute would amount to 6·4 per cent of the agricultural sector's income. By all indication, this is a minimal estimate. Given the certainty that P was greater than 1·67 in most years and the likely regressiveness of such a tax, it is highly probable that many smaller farmers were made to pay a concealed tax of more than 10 per cent of their incomes.

Thus we find that the peasants of pre-industrial Bangladesh have in recent times been subjected to a high rate of 'primitive capital accumulation' for the industrialisation of West Pakistan. This should give pause to those who would like to argue that, despite its poverty, agriculture in Bangladesh must bear the main burden of industrialisation; that simply because it is so large in relation to other sectors, the economy cannot have a high overall rate of accumulation unless agriculture is made to accumulate at a high rate to finance industrialisation.

PART II

The Present Structure of the Bangladesh Economy

4 The Transitional State of the Bangladesh Economy

4.1 THE CURRENT TRANSITION

THE Bangladesh economy is currently undergoing a major transition which makes it somewhat difficult to describe its present state. During the summer and autumn of 1971 there occurred a war of independence. The actions of the guerillas and the massive punitive reprisals by the Pakistan army created large-scale disruption in the life of the people of Bangladesh and resulted in significant damage to assets. Dislocation has almost certainly been disproportionate to the degree of firepower employed for the simple reason that Bangladesh was for the first time in its history experiencing modern war. Not in centuries had life been so massively disturbed. The turmoil reached a peak in December with the outbreak of an all-out war between India and Pakistan. During the three weeks of intense fighting before independence the transport and communications network suffered major damage, mainly due to the 'scorched earth' policy of the Pakistan army.

Since independence, inevitable structural and organisational changes have been taking place in the economy. The large regional trade with (West) Pakistan which had been created through high and discriminatory protection ceased completely. Since the production structure in Bangladesh was complementary to such regional trade, the economy has been faced with the short-term problem of supplies and adjustment. The opening up of trade with the giant neighbour, India, also creates a number of problems of adjustment. In the immediate future, the problem is one of adjusting to very different relative product prices since nothing but near free trade is feasible in view of the enormous open border. The ownership pattern in the organised sector is also undergoing drastic change. The Government of Bangladesh has emerged as the owner of all the enterprises

previously belonging to (West) Pakistani groups and indivi-
duals. This guarantees overwhelming public ownership of the
various organised parts of the economy.

Nor is the transition quite complete even in the organisational
aspects. Institutions are being set up and decisions taken and
revised almost every week. All these make the task of analysing
and quantifying the existing economic structure very difficult.

4.2 THE GAP IN KNOWLEDGE

In trying to fill in the important details with respect to the
various sectors and resources of the Bangladesh economy, we
are likely to face major difficulties. One set of such difficulties
derives from the generally inadequate knowledge about many
subsistence activities. The statistical knowledge about agriculture and its ancillary activities is incomplete and fragmentary.
The broad features of the overall pattern can roughly be drawn
once the large number of scattered surveys are analysed and the
diverse pieces from different sources put together. Inevitably,
however, some of the pieces of the enormous jig-saw puzzle
remain undiscovered while yet others do not appear to fit very
well together.

The other main gap is caused by the lack of definite quantitative information about the damage due to the war in 1971.
That much of the current output has been lost is beyond doubt.
The various output estimates in the following five chapters
would therefore not apply to the year 1971/72. It may indeed
take some time before pre-turmoil outputs are reached once
again.

A more important question is the extent to which productive
capacity has been lost due to the damage to physical assets.
Unless we can form some idea of the extent of such loss, we may
end up with a description, based on the statistics of recent years,
which has already been rendered completely unrepresentative
of the existing structure.

The manufacturing industries would appear to have sustained
relatively mild damage. The Bangladesh Industrial Development Corporation has prepared a detailed account of the
damage sustained by its enterprises. The total loss is evaluated
at nearly Rs. 99 million, but a very high proportion of it

consists of inventories, stores, chemicals, spares and furniture. Plant, machinery and directly productive fixed assets would be no more than 20 million rupees, which is probably about 3 per cent of the value of all the fixed assets owned by these industries. There is no reason to believe that the average proportion for the industrial sector as a whole has been any greater.

The traditional production technique in agriculture is some kind of an insurance against such damage. Although the pointless brutality of the Pakistan army led to at least partial destruction of nearly six million homes, according to the preliminary (and probably somewhat exaggerated) estimates of the Ministry of Rehabilitation, there is no reason to suppose that the output capacity in agriculture has suffered significant permanent damage. There is one important exception, however. It is not known to what extent livestock have been lost. Since animal-drawn ploughs are the nearly universal means of land preparation, the extent of such damage would largely determine productive capacity in near future.

The severest damage has been sustained by transport, communications and power transmission. Thus the description of the economic overheads in Chapter 7 probably constitutes a rather optimistic picture of today. The already overstretched facilities have today become one of the most important bottlenecks to be overcome and lack of capacity in this sector is a major short-term problem of transition.

Wherever possible in the following five chapters, we shall try to indicate the direction of organisational and structural change. The situation is, however, very fluid in certain areas. We shall try to suggest likely outcomes in such areas of great uncertainty. Even then, we are sure that quite a few of the descriptions in the following chapters will be rendered out of date during the gestation lag of the present work. It is, however, unlikely that our overall description will be a completely outdated characterisation of the organisation and structure of the Bangladesh economy today or even tomorrow when the dust settles down a bit more.

5 Agriculture

5.1 INTRODUCTION

THE dominant position of agriculture in the Bangladesh economy is expressed by the facts already discussed; it contributes more than 55 per cent to GDP and absorbs more than 75 per cent of the labour force. If the ancillary activities like transporting and marketing agricultural products are included, the sector's contribution to GDP would amount to more than two-thirds. Also the processing of domestically-produced agricultural goods accounts for well over half the value added in manufacturing industries.

And yet we have seen that in the past the sector was discriminated against. There was very little investment in agriculture. It was subjected to very heavy concealed taxation in addition to the moderate direct taxation of land and some less than successful attempts at taxing higher agricultural incomes. As a result the sector lagged seriously behind both the rest of the economy and the growth of population.

5.2 LAND TENURE AND OWNERSHIP DISTRIBUTION

The pattern of ownership distribution according to the 1960 Agricultural Census and the 1968 Master Survey of Agriculture (Seventh Round, Phase II) are shown in Table 5.1. Compared to the Agricultural Census, the more recent Master Survey shows a general decline in average farm size, leading to a higher proportion of small farms and a lower proportion of medium and large farms. This is partly explained by the fact that the Agricultural Census defines farm size as total area including both cultivated and uncultivated land, while the Master Survey defines it as cultivated area only. It is also likely that because of the inexorable operation of the inheritance law farm size declined significantly over an eight-year period during which population increased by nearly 30 per cent.

TABLE 5.1

DISTRIBUTION OF FARMS BY SIZE

Size of Farms in Acres	Agricultural Census 1960		Master Survey 1968	
	Percentage of Farm Area (1)	Percentage of Farms (2)	Percentage of Farm Area (3)	Percentage of Farms (4)
Under 1·0	3·24	24·31	4·24	24·96
1 to under 2·5	13·01	27·32	17·08	31·67
2·5 to under 5·0	26·40	26·31	29·97	26·32
5·0 to under 7·5	19·30	11·38	17·77	9·20
7·5 to under 12·5	19·14	7·21	15·52	5·25
12·5 to under 25·0	14·11	3·06	10·95	2·16
25·0 to under 40·0	2·91	0·35	3·30	0·36
40·0 and above	1·89	0·08	1·17	0·08

SOURCE
Cols. 1 and 2 estimated from the *Agricultural Census, 1960*, cols. 3 and 4 from the *Master Survey of East Pakistan Agriculture*, Seventh Round, Phase II.

According to the Agricultural Census, average farm size was 3·54 acres in 1960. Today it is very considerably smaller. Total cultivated area probably stands at 22·5 million acres. Applying the 1968 Master Survey estimates of farm households as percentage of rural households (73 per cent) and average rural family size (5·65) to our benchmark rural population, we get an estimate of 8·69 million agricultural families (including those owning no land). Average size turns out to be 2·59 acres per agricultural household (including the non-owning ones). Taking only the owning farm households, the average would be 3·14 acres.

The striking feature of the ownership distribution is that a vast proportion of farms are small by any standard while a very small proportion can really be regarded as big. According to the 1968 Survey only 30,000 farms are bigger than 25 acres. Together they account for less than 4½ per cent of cultivable land.

On the other hand, it would not make sense to continue to be guided by the conventional notion of bigness, derived in the context of a substantially more favourable land/man ratio, when the average size is only 2·59 acres and nearly two-thirds of the farms are below average in size. The ownership distribution, judged on the basis of the measure of skewness, is highly unequal upwards. In the given context, those with three to four times the average size must be treated as very large indeed!

To complete the picture of the ownership pattern, we need to know the proportion of the households without any land whatsoever – the rural proletariat. Unfortunately no published information is available from the Agricultural Census or Master Survey. The most recent estimate known to the present writer is based on the 1966 Agricultural Credit Survey which, on the basis of a survey of 1234 families in twelve villages in twelve districts all over Bangladesh, puts the proportion at 6·97 per cent.[1] The variance of the cross-section of the ratio is rather high; the ratio is as low as 1·41 per cent in Natore (Lakshmipur village) and as high as 17·31 per cent in Goalunda (Bishnupur). For a land-poor country, the average ratio is strikingly low. But there is no strong statistical evidence to cast serious doubt on the estimate. In fact, there is a good deal of corroborative evidence. Thus the Master Survey of 1968 shows 'agricultural labourers' as only 8·61 per cent of the rural population of age ten and above. Since 'agricultural operators', family workers and all other possible categories have been shown separately, these must refer to the landless labourers. Thus the figure of 6·97 per cent for 1966 does not appear to be particularly suspect although the proportion may have gone up a little by now for demographic reasons.

To look at another aspect of the land system, summarised in Table 5.2, an overwhelming proportion of farms are either owner-operated or owner-cum-tenant operated. A negligible proportion of farms are operated by landless farmers on a sharecropping or renting basis.

One curious aspect of the system is that the average size of the owner-cum-tenant operated farms is very much larger than that of the owner-operated farms. It seems that the medium owners operate as farmers on their own land while a good many

[1] Registrar of Co-operative Societies, *Agricultural Credit in East Pakistan, January, 1966 – A Survey Report* (Dacca, 1967).

of the larger owners rent out their land to be operated by smaller owners and, to a very small extent, by landless farmers. Thus, it would appear that large ownership tends to result in greater resort to sharecropping than to capitalist farming based on modern technology – a phenomenon we shall come back to in our discussion of agricultural planning.

TABLE 5.2

ASPECTS OF LAND TENURE

(A)		(B)	
Type of Tenure	*Percentage of farms*	*Type of Tenure*	*Percentage of of Area*
Owner operated farms	61	Owner operated farms	82
Owner-cum-Tenant farms	37	Tenant operated:	18
Tenant farms	2	Sharecropping (16)	
		Cash Renting (2)	

(C)	
Average Size of	*Acres*
Owner operated farms	3·1
Owner-cum-Tenant farms	4·3
Tenant farms	2·4

SOURCE
1960 Pakistan Census of Agriculture, A Summary of East Pakistan Data.

Distribution of ownership is, however, no index of the size distribution of the consolidated operating units. This is because of the extensive fragmentation of holdings. Ninety-six per cent of farm land is held in fragmented holdings. Table 5.3 shows the situation according to the 1960 Agricultural Census. Today it must be even worse.

Only about 10 per cent of farms and 4 per cent of farm land are unfragmented. A higher proportion of larger farms are fragmented as compared to small farms. It would clearly be misleading to think that bigger ownership units also mean equally bigger consolidated operating units.

How widely prevalent is sharecropping? A decade ago, no more than 16 per cent of the total land area was operated under this system. In the discussion of agricultural development, this system is frequently identified with inefficiency. The argument is that it resembles a system of very high proportional taxation and hence is responsible for a great deal of disincentive on the part of the operator. While the system is prevalent over a significant proportion of land area, it can certainly not be described as the dominant mode of production.[1]

TABLE 5.3

FRAGMENTATION OF FARMS IN BANGLADESH

Number of Fragments per Farm	*Per cent of Total Number of Farms*
Non-fragmented	10
2–3 fragments	21
4–5 fragments	17
6–9 fragments	23
10 or more fragments	29

Fragmentation of Different Sizes of Farms	*Fragmented Farms as Percentage of All Farms in the Size Class*
Small Farms (less than 2·5 acres)	83
Medium-sized Farms (2·5 to 12·5 acres)	97
Large farms (12·5 acres and more)	97

The land tenure and ownership pattern may be summarised as follows: for a country with such low land/man ratio, Bangladesh has a surprisingly low proportion of landless farmers. However, there is a massive proportion of 'near landless' farmers. Also, there is a considerable degree of inequality in so far as over 30 per cent of land is held in ownership units three times or more than the average size of ownership. It appears that the larger owners tend to let land out for share-cropping to small farmers and that such arrangements cover a significant, though not overwhelming, proportion of cultivated land.

5.3 LAND UTILISATION AND CROPPING PATTERN

Table 5.4 summarises the patterns of cropping and land use in the recent past. One of the things to note is that in spite of a

[1] It is possible that there might have been some bias in under-reporting sharecropping but this speculation is not based on detailed knowledge of the situation.

great scarcity of land, cropping intensity is not all that high. Only about 35 per cent of the area is cropped more than once on the average. Compared to this is the fact that the extensive margin has virtually been reached in using land.

It would, however, be incorrect to think that the country has excess capacity of cropped acreage. The early rainy season crop is subject to a great deal of flooding, and both flooding and overlap make it impossible for each of the rainy season crops to expand in acreage. An expansion in acreage in these seasons is possible only through flood control and drainage. During the dry season, however, a very small proportion of land is used. Here the possibility of expansion would appear to be quite large if and only if irrigation is provided. In the absence of a hydrological survey, it is impossible to know the extent to which cropped acreage in winter can be expanded. On the indication of the rudimentary information that can be assembled on the availability of surface and groundwater, it appears that considerable expansion can be made.

On the other hand, it would be wrong to believe that land scarcity is imaginary. For one thing, acreage expansion involves considerable investment in irrigation which is expensive and hence must be weighed against the alternative ways of obtaining output, e.g. increasing yield through the use of fertiliser, pesticide etc. More important, even after irrigation is provided, there will be very limited opportunity for triple cropping for sheer lack of time. This is particularly true for improved seed varieties like IRRI which require a longer germination period. Much of any additional boro rice will inevitably mean forgoing aus crop to the extent that land was suitable for the latter.

The actual estimate of acreage expansion possibilities cannot be made for want of information on water availability in the dry season, possible overlap in growing periods of various crops and varieties and a host of other factors. It appears however that it would be far too optimistic to hope for a cropping intensity of 200 per cent.

Agriculture is overwhelmingly dominated by rice, the crop around which the entire economic life gravitates.[1] Rice cultiva-

[1] In Bangladesh the standard way of enquiring whether someone has eaten is to ask, 'Have you taken rice?'

TABLE 5.4

LAND UTILISATION AND CROPPING PATTERN IN BANGLADESH
averages for three years, 1966/67 to 1968/69

	Aus (early rainy season)	Rice Aman. (main rainy season)	Boro (dry season)	Total Rice	Jute (early rainy season)	Sugarcane (perennial)	Oilseeds (dry season)	Others (all seasons)	Total cropped acreage
Million acres	7·61	14·38	1·65	23·64	2·32	0·10	0·79	3·39	30·24
% of cropped acreage	25·17	47·55	5·46	78·18	7·67	0·33	2·61	11·21	100·00
% of cultivated acreage	33·87	64·00	7·34	105·21	10·32	0·45	3·52	15·09	134·58

NOTE

Cropping intensity, defined as total cropped acreage as percentage of cultivated acreage, is shown in the last column, last row entry. It would be higher if defined, as is done sometimes, as the percentage of net area sown (i.e. cultivated area less current fallow).

Total acreage is 22·47 million.

Total cropped acreage is average for 1966/67 and 1967/68 only. Source: Government of Pakistan (Ministry of Agriculture and Works), *Agricultural Statistics of Pakistan*, Fact Series no. vi, January 1970, and I.B.R.D., *Proposals For an Action Program: East Pakistan Agriculture and Water Development*, July 1970 (mimeographed).

tion covers nearly 80 per cent of the cropped acreage. In recent years, output of rice has been reported to have been in the neighbourhood of 11·5 million tons. This has been less than what was needed for domestic consumption. Imports over the five-year period ending in 1968/69 have been at an annual average rate of 0·37 million tons.

It would, however, be wrong to conclude that the deficit of consumption over production can be covered by producing an additional amount equal to imports. First, over the last decade, a part of rice consumption has been replaced by wheat consumption. The consumption of wheat has been met by imports which have been cheaper than rice imports. While the consumption preference has always been in favour of rice, the absorption of some wheat has been possible through an extremely favourable shift in relative prices. Any sensible target of self-sufficiency should aim at the import substitution of wheat as well. Since it is unlikely that the relative cost advantage for wheat (which is a very small crop in Bangladesh) would be greater than the relative consumer preference for rice, it would appear that the current import of wheat will have to be replaced by the expansion of rice output. Since wheat imports stood at an annual average of 0·77 million tons over the five years ending 1968/69, it would appear that the current deficit would be about 1·14 million tons or 10 per cent of current rice production. Secondly, we have already noted in Chapter 3 that 45 per cent of the population suffer from a calorie deficiency and so future planning must attach great priority to raising these people above the starvation level. This factor would probably raise the self-sufficiency level by another 5 per cent or so. Thus apart from the need to have a sustained growth of 3 to 5 per cent per year to keep pace with population and increasing income per head, there is the need for a once-for-all jump of about 15 per cent unless foreign exchange is to be wasted for imports of rice.

We shall approach the problem of how best to plan for the required increase in rice output later. Here it may simply be pointed out that a comparison of yield per acre shows that Bangladesh is very nearly at the bottom (Table 5.5).

Even many of the South Asian countries with not too different geographical and human circumstances have very significantly greater yields. If, for example, Bangladesh can only approach the per acre yield in war-torn Vietnam, the entire deficit can be wiped out. While the backwardness itself is depressing, it is also a source of optimism in so far as the examples of other countries show that it should be possible to go a very long way.

TABLE 5·5

INDEX OF RICE-YIELD PER ACRE IN SELECTED COUNTRIES DURING 1965 TO 1967

(Bangladesh = 100)

Australia	410	South Vietnam	119
Spain	372	Ceylon	116
Japan	319	Indonesia	114
Egypt	298	North Vietnam	111
USA	297	Thailand	101
Italy	281	India	96
Korea	244	Burma	96
Taiwan	241		
China	152	Europe	270
		Near East	188
		Far East (Except China)	106

NOTE

Data for all countries except Bangladesh have been taken from FAO, *Production Yearbook* 1968 and are averages for 1965, 1966 and 1967 (for China the data refer to 1952–56 and for India to the average for 1964 and 1967). Bangladesh data are for 1965/66, 1966/67 and 1967/68 and the source is the same as in Table 5.4 above.

Jute, though completely dwarfed by rice in terms of share of acreage, is equally overwhelming in importance in a different context. In raw or manufactured form it has earned nearly 90 per cent of foreign exchange for Bangladesh. It is the principal cash crop for the Bengali peasants and its price has been the single most important determinant of the non-subsistence consumption of the rural population. Its foreign exchange earnings have financed much of Pakistan's industrialisation in the fifties and sixties. And yet through the whole period, jute was systematically discriminated against. The discrimination was enforced through a very high effective taxation on producers concealed in the form of an unfavourable rate of exchange and export tax. The *de facto* embargo on trade with India, precipitated by the Pakistan government's policy soon after independence, forced India into import substitution of raw jute. This was a positive hindrance to the growth of jute production in Bangladesh. With the Bangladesh jute manufacturing industry dominated by West Pakistani owners, the policy of the Pakistani authorities aimed at achieving the dual objective of keeping the domestic rupee price of raw jute low and deriving the maximum short-term advantage by forcing on the foreign buyers as high a foreign exchange price as possible. This was achieved by imposing on jute the lowest of all the effective rates of exchange existing in the country's external trade. By 1970 a dollar earned by raw jute export had to be surrendered for Rs. 4·75 whereas a dollar earned by most other exports was being exchanged for over Rs. 8.[1]

Largely as a result of all these policies, the share of Bangladesh gradually fell to around 50 per cent from the virtual monopoly in the world export of jute and substitute fibres. Domestically, jute production stagnated and output per acre declined (from an average of 0.64 tons per acre in the early sixties to an average of 0·54 in the late sixties, according to official statistics). But in spite of these unfavourable circumstances, Bangladesh continues to have an edge over the next biggest producer, India, in terms of per acre productivity of jute (Table 5.6).

TABLE 5.6

PER ACRE OUTPUT OF RAW JUTE IN TONS

Year	India	Bangladesh
1964/65	·515	·573
1965/66	·425	·544
1966·67	·482	·580
1967/68	·515	·552
1968/69	·414	·473
Average	·470	·544

SOURCE
Commonwealth Economic Committee, *Industrial Fibres*, 1970.

Now that the trade between Bangladesh and India has been restored and their is a favourable prospect that trade will grow rapidly it would make sense for India to re-examine the costly

[1] This was being done through the export bonus scheme. See Chapter 8 for an explanation and the estimation of the effective rate of exchange.

import substitution made under the conditions of trade embargo. A crude estimate of 'comparative advantage' shows that
India would do better to shift away from jute (where its output
per acre is 16 per cent lower than in Bangladesh) to, say, rice
(where its output per acre is nearly the same as in Bangladesh).[1]

After rice and jute, the important crops are various kinds of
pulses and oilseeds, sugarcane, tobacco and tea. Each of them is
small in relation to the two crops discussed above. Tea, unlike
any other agricultural activity, is not competitive with other
crops in land use. The remaining crops, though important, are
not thought to present as important problems of choice as do
the ones above.

5.4 TECHNOLOGY IN AGRICULTURE

The low yield per acre in agriculture is due mainly to the backward technology used. Through the generations, there has been
little change in technical means of cultivation and the overall
technology today is only marginally different from what it was
a century ago. Our characterisation of the technology as backward is not due to the predominance of bullock ploughs and the
near absence of the modern 'mechanical-engineering' technology. Such technology being usually associated with labour
replacement, one would not worry too much about its absence
in a labour-abundant economy.[2] It is the lack of advance in the
adoption of the 'biological-chemical' technology (which is
associated with rising yield per acre) and irrigation (which
increases the supply of land by increasing the cropping intensity) that is believed to have been the limiting factor in the
situation of extreme scarcity of land.

As shown in Table 5.7, irrigation covers only about 4 per cent

---

[1] This is merely an illustration. It is not suggested that Bangladesh should
export jute to India to import rice from the latter. India could probably use
the rice herself and sell Bangladesh some of the goods which she now sells
abroad to pay for her rice (or other grain imports).

[2] This does not mean that it is unreasonable to want to learn whether
and/or for how long the use of some types of mechanical devices must be
postponed in view of the shortage of time between crops, the scarcity of
land to grow fodder and similar other considerations. All that is being said
is that mechanisation which merely replaces labour by machines does not
seem to be an economically sensible policy.

of the cultivated acreage. Although the monsoon land of Bangladesh is pictured in the popular mind as a water-submerged country, it has a long dry season when cropping can be done only with irrigation, except in a very few low-lying areas. Dry-season rice is cultivated on only 7 per cent of the available land, and together with low-water-requiring crops which are cultivated in this season, accounts for not much more than 10 per cent of the land. In the mid-sixties, low-lift pumps were introduced, partly to sidetrack the problem of flood control, as a low-cost method of expanding cropping intensity. Ever since, this has been the main thrust of winter irrigation. Though by 1970 this system had come to command more than 75 per cent of modern irrigation, its growth can by no means be called spectacular when compared with total acreage.

TABLE 5.7

IRRIGATED AREA IN 1969/70

Name of Project	Thousand Acres
Water and Power Development Authority	
Ganges-Kobadak Phase I	90
Teesta Barrage	6
Northern Tubewells	62
Northern Lift Pumps	10
Dacca-Narayanganj-Demra	9
Agricultural Development Corporation	
Low Lift Pumps (18,000)	720
Tubewells	22
Comilla Co-operatives	8
Total	927 (4% of cultivated area)

SOURCE
I.B.R.D., op. cit. (compiled from Planning and Agriculture Departments). Excludes tanks, traditional wells and small traditional canals for which estimates are not available.

The rate of fertiliser distribution is shown in Table 5.8. In recent years the average dose has been no more than 10 lb nutrient per acre. This is perhaps no more than one-thirtieth of the desired dose. Since the fertiliser users are known to spread it too thinly,[1] the situation is worse than it would be if the same amount of fertiliser were used over a much smaller area. Most farms are by a great distance inside the point of inflection of the returns to fertiliser curve so that their experience is unlikely to do much good to the cause of spreading the use of this vital input. Another point to note is that the fertiliser distribution programme started out by over-emphasising urea (nitrogen), due perhaps to its availability from domestic production. The exclusive use of nitrogen can be very dangerous to crops. Although the sale of other types has increased in recent years, urea still seems to have an unhealthy preponderance.

TABLE 5.8

DISTRIBUTION OF FERTILISER
(thousand tons)

	Urea	T.S.P.	Super phosphate	Potash	Amm. Sulph.	Total	Nutrient Tons
1960/61	30·38	6·50	—	1·65	27·38	65·92	23·72
1961/62	29·02	5·99	1·65	1·03	29·27	66·95	23·19
1962/63	41·12	3·09	2·52	1·97	24·53	73·23	27·12
1963/64	75·03	22·99	2·02	4·12	7·56	111·72	49·50
1964/65	71·06	18·97	0·34	3·93	7·32	101·59	45·37
1965/66	83·31	20·47	0·10	3·82	21·33	129·03	54·52
1966/67	120·87	34·46	0·06	8·31	6·23	169·93	77·76
1967/68	151·92	48·10	0·02	11·48	15·41	226·93	102·13
1968/69	159·94	52·00	0·02	12·43	12·12	237·45	105·49
1969/70	200·00	65·00	—	20·00	15·00	300·00	134·40

SOURCE
Planning Department, *East Pakistan Economic Survey 1969/70* (Dacca, 1970).

At the time when 'green revolutions' in a number of Asian countries were being spearheaded by the changeover to improved seed, the rate of progress in the distribution of this major source of increased productivity in agriculture has been the most unimpressive. The amount of improved seed available

[1] See S. R. Bose, 'East-West Contrast in Pakistan's Agricultural Development,' in Keith Griffin and A. R. Khan (eds), *Growth and Inequality in Pakistan* (Macmillan, 1972).

through imports and production by registered seed growers is shown in Table 5.9.

TABLE 5.9

IMPROVED SEED DISTRIBUTION AND PLANT PROTECTION

	Thousand Maunds of Seed		Acres Receiving Plant Protection (million)
	Paddy	Jute	
1963/64	51·2	1·0	2·8
1964/65	51·9	1·5	4·6
1965/66	58·3	1·4	5·3
1967/68	59·7	2·2	7·4
1968/69	60·0	4·0	8·2 (projection)
1969/70	72·0	8·5	10·0 (projection)

SOURCE
Seed distribution from Planning Department, *East Pakistan Economic Survey 1969–70* (Dacca, 1970). Plant protection from Government of East Pakistan Plant Protection Department.

To the extent that unregistered growers have been producing to use and/or sell improved varieties, our figures may be an underestimate. But such production does not seem to have been very much, nor would it make much difference to the above conclusion even if it is large in relation to the reported quantity. By 1969–70 improved paddy seeds were a mere 0·5 per cent of the total paddy seeds used. For jute, the share was a little better but still under 3 per cent of the total.

While the negligible proportion of improved paddy seeds consists of improved traditional varieties and imported IRRI (developed at and named after the International Rice Research Institute, Los Baños, Philippines) varieties, little effort has been made in the direction of basic research in developing new varieties suited to the land conditions and factor supply situation. The small amount of seed research is almost exclusively concerned with the trials and assessments of various imported improved varieties.

The hot and humid climate of Bangladesh fosters crop pests and diseases of many kinds. Under 'normal' pest incidence, the loss of crop is estimated to be between 10 and 15 per cent. In these circumstances it would appear to be a particularly vulnerable situation that less than a third of the acreage today receives any kind of plant protection. Moreover, the protection, even where it is available, is often too thin and not always disease-specific. The lack of plant protection is certainly one of the major contributions to high variance in crop yields which leads to so much of uncertainty facing the production decisions of the average farmers.

From the account above, it should be clear that Bangladesh had little experience of the green revolution in the recent past. It has lagged behind even in relation to its subcontinental neighbours during the decade that witnessed the discovery of miracle seeds which led to remarkable yield increases, especially when complementary fertiliser, pesticide and water inputs were provided.

What were the major reasons for the failure of Bangladesh agriculture to achieve even a mild rate of technological advance? The first explanatory characteristic lies in the ownership pattern in agriculture. As discussed earlier, very few of the farms were big enough to generate an internal surplus which could finance the acquisition of knowledge and purchase of technology. The problem could perhaps be resolved by a massive public sector effort towards the provision of agricultural extension and credit to finance working capital needs for the adoption of improved technology. Little advance was made in these directions.

It remains, however, to be explained why technological advance did not take place among the bigger farms. About 15 per cent of the cultivable area was held in ownership units of more than twelve acres. There is no indication that significant advance was made by these larger farms. The weight of evidence, though by no means conclusive, would appear to support the opposite hypothesis in so far as even quite recent surveys reveal that per acre output is more often a declining function of farm size.

We have already referred to the tentative conclusion that larger ownership unit is not associated with larger entrepreneurship, that bigger operators are only part-owners and part-tenants of land belonging to bigger owners. It would appear that agriculture in Bangladesh is an example of the relevance of the hypothesis that larger ownership merely converts a family to an altogether different status which is non-entrepreneurial in the given context. Thus a five-acre household may be reconciled to farming as the major occupation while a twenty-acre household would be considered a part of the rural gentry for whom manual work or field supervision would be considered too undignified. It would end up entering into a sharecropping arrangement with one or more five-acre farmers who would have farming know-how, implements, bullocks and some surplus family labour.

Perhaps the larger owners would see the opportunity of organising the farm on capitalistic lines based on modern technology if their holdings were much bigger and they had better urban connections and a good deal of education. But a look at the frequency distribution of ownership is enough to be convinced that few farms were above such threshold size.

One final point needs to be noted. Output per acre is not only low but also subject to a high standard deviation. One of the causes, plant disease and epidemics, has already been noted. The most important factor however is flood, which introduces a random element of disproportionate magnitude. In such a situation, the farmers, particularly the vast multitude of small farmers, would be unwilling to undertake much investment even if knowledge were available and much of the required capital were provided from outside at reasonable rates of interest. We shall discuss the problem of flooding in Chapter 7.

5.5 AGRICULTURAL CREDIT

Because of the great importance of credit in financing the working capital needs of farmers, it is useful to examine the current state of affairs with respect to its availability and use. The available information is summarised in Table 5.10. Nearly half the households in need of credit had access to no source during the year under review.

Those who succeeded in getting credit were still left with more than a third of their requirement unfulfilled. Thus clearly a great deal of excess demand for credit exists in rural Bangladesh.

TABLE 5.10

STATISTICS ON RURAL CREDIT

Percentage of families having some debt		53·7%
Average debt per *indebted* household		Rs. 275
Percentage of families borrowing last year		45·9%
Average loan by borrowing families last year		Rs. 201
Sources of loan:		
Institutional		13·86%
(of which Taccavi	0·77%	
ADB	5·36%	
Co-operative	7·73%)	
Rural rich		52·06%
Friends and relatives		25·59%
Others		8·49%
Use of loan:		
Capital expenditure on farm		24·03%
Current expenditure on farm		18·73%
Non-farm expenditure		9·21%
Family Expenditure		48·03%
Annual requirement of loan per loan-requiring family		Rs. 309
Percentage of families requiring loan		80·7%

SOURCE
The Registrar of Co-operative Societies, *Agricultural Credit in East Pakistan, A Survey Report* (Dacca, 1967).

A second feature of the credit scene is the small proportion of total borrowing that is used for directly 'productive purposes'. About half the credit is for consumption purposes with nearly another tenth for non-agricultural use. Thus it would appear that working capital in agriculture is needed not only to finance direct input purchases but also to pay at least partly for the consumption by the family labour. This only shows the extent of extreme poverty in rural Bangladesh. It would also be misleading to think that a credit programme can do away with this so-called consumption demand for credit. It only shows that the farmers require credit to 'pay' wages to the family labourers during the long gestation period. It is no more a consumption loan than the borrowing by industries for working capital requirements.

Another feature of the credit situation is the extremely low share of all the institutional sources put together, less than a seventh. Even ignoring the possibility that the farmers' own assessment of credit requirement is an underestimate because they are unaware of the potential investment opportunities, the institutional sources satisfy no more than 5 per cent of all credit *needs*.[1] Thus the role of institutional credit in removing bottlenecks from agricultural financing have indeed been negligible.

It would appear that much of agricultural borrowing is short-term. Nearly two-thirds of the outstanding indebtedness in January 1966 was contracted over the one-year period preceding that date.

There is nothing directly known about the overall cost of credit to the farmer. With the possible exception of friends and relatives, however, it would appear that the institutional sources have been the cheapest. Co-operative credit is the biggest of the institutional sources both in terms of overall and incremental shares. In recent years they charged an interest of 9 per cent. But making allowance for the facts that 10 per cent of the lending had to be deposited in the Co-operative Bank to open a deposit account and that a part of the loan was converted into kind irrespective of whether the farmer wanted or not, it would be realistic to put the interest rate at over 10 per cent. This is probably still less than the social cost of capital, but it has to be recognised that this has been considerably in excess of the rate at which industries were able to borrow from the banking system.[2]

But the average cost of credit to the agriculturalists must have been much higher. The 'rich and well-to-do' in the village, which is a euphemism for moneylenders, have certainly been lending at a much higher rate of interest. Also it appears certain that the extortionate moneylenders have been the residual sources of credit, that the better-off farmers have found

---

[1] Calculated as follows: 56·8 per cent of those farmers who need credit have 65 per cent of their needs satisfied. Thus 36·9 per cent of all needs are satisfied. The share of institutional credit is 13·8 per cent of the available amount or 5·11 per cent of the needed amount.

[2] During the 1960s, the weighted annual average of interest rates on advances by banks to the industries ranged between 5 and 7·5 per cent. see the relevant issue of the State Bank of Pakistan's *Bulletin*.

it easier to have access to institutional credit and that the relatively smaller and poorer ones have more often been left with the moneylenders as the last resort. Thus there seems to be little doubt that the cost of credit has been very high, particularly for the smaller farmers, perhaps higher than the value of credit to the society and certainly several times the price the big industrialists paid.

6 The Structure of Manufacturing Industries

6.1 SOURCES OF INFORMATION

THREE kinds of surveys have been available for Bangladesh industries. For the large- and medium-scale modern manufacturing units, the Ministry of Industries carries out censuses of manufacturing industries (CMI). The latest available (though yet unpublished) CMI is for the year 1967/68 and it goes back to 1954 with occasional gaps for some years. For most years the information is available separately for the so-called '2(j) industries' (those units employing twenty or more workers *and* using power) and the '5(1) industries' (those units employing 10 or more persons without the use of power and between 10 and 19 workers with the use of power).[1]

The then East Pakistan Small Industries Corporation carried out a survey of small-scale industries (SSI) for the year 1963/64 which provides a comprehensive account of all units having a value of fixed assets not exceeding Rs. 250,000. The definition of the small-scale industrial units in terms of the value of fixed assets and of the CMI industries in terms of employment makes it difficult to ascertain the extent of overlap, if any, particularly between the 5(1) and the small-scale enterprises. It is, however, found that the average value of fixed assets of the 5(1) units reported in the CMI is only a small fraction of the upper limit of SSI; it is only 25·6 thousand for the year 1967/68. A careful examination of the four-digit sector classification of 5(1) industries shows that it is unlikely that any single unit is too large to be included under the SSI definition. The CMI coverage of the 5(1) industries is a small proportion of the SSI coverage, indicating perhaps that the greater proportion of the SSI consists of units employing less than 10 – a plausible explanation in

---

[1] The names are derived from the respective clauses of the Factories Act which defines them.

view of an average of eight workers in these units. It would be reasonable to assume that SSI covers all 5(1) units for the relevant year.

The Small Industries Corporation also published a Survey of Cottage Industries (SCI) showing the state of the industries which are 'carried on wholly or mainly by the members of a family either as a whole-time or as a part-time occupation' during the calendar year 1962. The definition of these industries leaves little scope for any overlap with the other classes discussed above.

We shall follow the convention of calling the 2(j) industries in the CMI large-scale, the SSI industries small-scale and the SCI industries cottage industries. Together the three classes would appear to be co-extensive and without any significant overlap.

The SSI and SCI have not been repeated in recent years so that our information would appear to be outdated. On the other hand these industries, particularly the SCI ones, had a very slow rate of growth so that they are not altogether misleading pictures of their present selves. The large-scale industries have grown more rapidly and for them our information is more up-to-date.

It is important to recognise that the CSO national income estimates shown in Chapter 3 make little use of the censuses and surveys noted above. They use the CMI only for 1959/60, after which they find large-scale industries' value-added by applying a dubious index of industrial production (*not* of real value-added). For small-scale industry, they apply net income per worker (postulated from indirect information on wages for rural areas and based on a survey of Karachi, West Pakistan, for urban areas) to the estimated labour force. It appears strange that no effort has been made to incorporate the only available direct information!

6.2 DUALISM IN INDUSTRY

The national accounts show that the large-scale industries in recent years have contributed two-thirds of the value added in manufacturing. But the economy is still very considerably dependent on small and cottage industries. In fact the dependence is very much greater in terms of employment and in terms of the supply of the most important non-food consumption good, cloth. Even in recent years, cottage industries' share in the output of cloth has been 64 per cent and small industries' 26 per cent, leaving the large-scale industries with only 10 per cent (not counting imports).

An attempt at comparing the three types of manufacturing is made in Table 6.1. They are so vastly different that it would appear to serve little useful purpose in treating them as a homogeneous activity. Cottage industries, in particular, stand out as a very different kind of activity as compared to the others, which have important differences between them. Cottage industries are family-based enterprises, using negligible hired wage-labour and operating within residential homes. In their organisation they resemble agriculture rather than industry, although their output is mainly for sale and not for self-consumption, which is more often the case with subsistence agriculture. Their technology is almost entirely traditional, which is an additional point of similarity with agriculture and of difference from industry.

Cottage industries employ more than three times the labour force in large- and small-scale industries taken together. But there is little reason to think that the nature of employment is similar to that in others. Output per worker in these industries is extremely low. At Rs. 270 per year, it was just about one-ninth of that in small-scale and one-twentieth of that in large-scale industries. What is even more surprising is that output per worker in cottage industries is almost a third of the wage rate in small-scale and almost a fifth of that in large-scale industries. If demand for labour were at all elastic at the going wage rate in the latter industries, it would be impossible to explain the continued operation of the cottage enterprises.

Also such dismally low productivity could hardly be possible if the labour force were fully employed in any sense. There inevitably exists a good deal of work-sharing imposed by the shortage of physical capital, shortage in the supply of raw material (e.g. that of yarn for the handloom weaving industry) and even shortage and/or seasonality of demand. Like agriculture, cottage industries would appear to be a residual employment category.

Value-added per worker differs greatly, by nearly a factor of $2\frac{1}{2}$, between large-scale and small-scale industries. The difference between wages is less, that in small-scale being 60 per cent of large-scale. Once again, the picture is one of a great deal of market imperfection and inflexibility so that vastly different types are able to coexist. Although the difference between large- and small-scale industry is not as great as that between these industries and the cottage ones, the difference is so large in absolute terms that it makes sense to describe the situation as one of triangularism rather than dualism.

Let us explore some of the other features of the triangularism in industries. Capital-intensity is highest for the large-scale and lowest for the cottage industries. It is, however, important to note that, as capital-intensity increases between cottage and small-scale industry, so does labour productivity in about the same proportion, leaving the capital-output ratio roughly the same. The comparison between small-scale and large-scale brings out an altogether different picture: more than seven times higher capital-intensity in large-scale is associated with only a less than two-and-a-half times higher labour productivity. As a consequence, the capital-output ratio in large-scale industries is nearly three times as high as that in small-scale.[1]

A proper analysis of the relative efficiency of factor use by the three types of industries would require the isolation of factors like differences in product composition, distortions in relative prices and heterogeneity of measurements in the three sectors. Putting these factors aside for the moment, it would appear that the scarce factor, capital, was being more efficiently used by small-scale industries than by large-scale. This is true both for aggregate industries and for detailed sectors. Also, the advantage of the small-scale industries is in terms of both higher

[1] For large-scale industries in Table 6.1 capital refers to the book value of fixed assets. As we shall demonstrate later, this involves an understatement because depreciation allowances have been far greater than physical deterioration, and prices have been rising. The SSI and SCI do not explain clearly whether such understatement exists in them as well. It appears that in these surveys direct estimate of replacement value has been attempted, so that there would be no systematic bias although error may be significant. Had we used real value of capital (i.e. estimated replacement cost) for large-scale industries, the conclusions in this section would be strengthened further.

TABLE 6.1

COMPARISON OF LARGE, SMALL AND COTTAGE INDUSTRIES

	Large	Small	Cottage
Value-added per worker (Rs.)	5706	2336	270
Capital/Value-added ratio	1·734	0·583	0·552
Capital/Labour ratio (Rs.)	9892	1363	149
Workers per unit	191	8·15	3·3
Hired workers per unit	All	Most	0·3
Family labour per unit	None	Negligible	3·0
Employment as % of civilian labour force	0·9% (1967/68)	0·9% (1963/64)	5·9% (1962/63)
Annual wage per workers (Rs.)	1268	761*	—
Wage per unit of capital	0·128	0·558	—
'Surplus' per unit of capital†	0·449	1·156	—

* For 5(1) industries shown in the CMI since SSI does not have any estimate.

† Surplus refers to value-added less wages and includes depreciation and capitalists' consumption. Even if these were measurable, it is unlikely that surplus per unit of capital would be less for small-scale once these were excluded.

current output and higher investible surplus.[1] Although wages are much higher proportions of net output and capital in small-scale industries, the very low capital requirement per unit of output offsets these phenomena. Thus irrespective of whether the society wants to maximise current output or the growth rate of output in the immediate future (or any combination of them), the small-scale industries would appear to have a definite advantage over the large-scale (unless of course the nature of the product dictates the scale and/or the factors noted above as qualifications become dominating factors). To epitomise their

[1] One may wonder why private investment was concentrated in large-scale if the rate of profit was higher in small-scale industry. Once again, a full explanation will have to entail not only economic but also a lot of other considerations. This is somewhat beyond our ability to investigate at this stage. We would, however, like to enumerate a few factors. Private profit in large-scale industry would be higher than shown above if one were to include the gains from over-invoicing, scarcity premium of import licenses, cheap bank credit and so on. These opportunities were available only to the owners of the large enterprises. To these must be added the consideration of power and influence derived from the ownership of the large units.

comparative performance, the large-scale industries may be characterised as using up a great deal of capital to employ a small number of workers and provide them with a standard of living which is fairly close to the average for the nation as a whole, and as generating an investible surplus of less than half the value of the capital used up. In contrast the small-scale industries employ more than seven times as many workers with the same amount of capital, provide them with a standard of living more than a third *below* the national average; and yet generate more than two-and-a-half times as much investible surplus.

In comparing the efficiency of factor use between small-scale and cottage industries, we find that the capital intensity in the latter is a small fraction of the former but that this is almost wholly offset by lower labour productivity, so that the capital-output ratios in the two sectors are roughly the same. It does not make sense to try to distinguish between wages and profits in the value-added in cottage industries, but it would appear unlikely that at such dismally low incomes any significant investible surplus will be left over. Thus it would appear that in the cottage industries, the same amount of capital as in small-scale industries is used to produce roughly the same quantity of output to be divided among a great many more workers with little or no investible surplus left. Thus, while the cottage industries have no advantage over small-scale with respect to current output, they are at a great disadvantage with respect to the growth of output in the immediate future.

On first approximation, it would appear that the small-scale industries make the most efficient use of capital. In large-scale industry, there is too heavy a distribution of capital among workers, resulting in too little current output. In the cottage industries capital is so thinly distributed among workers as to leave little surplus of output over current consumption of the workers.

What modification do we have to make in our first approximation if some of the abstractions made earlier are removed by the substitution of realistic considerations? First, we have to consider the assumption that the three alternative techniques are available for all goods. This is partly untrue. Fertiliser can probably be produced only in large-scale factories and in general, despite the Chinese demonstration to the contrary, steel will probably not be produced in the backyard. But for many products the assumption will hold at least to the extent that small-scale technique can produce many things that are produced in the large-scale industries, although cottage industries may be able to produce only a relatively small number of goods produced by large-scale industry. As Table 6.2 shows, the transition from small-scale production to large-scale sometimes implies a significant difference in the nature of the product (e.g. the changing of consumption pattern from bidi to cigarettes and from brown sugar to white crystal sugar), but in many cases the difference would be negligible (e.g. in cotton textiles, metal products, wood and furniture, leather products and so on).

In Table 6.2 the sectoral capital-output ratios for large-scale industries have been adjusted for the understatement of book values in relation to real values[1] and the resulting figures, representing the real magnitudes more accurately, lend support to the above conclusions quite strongly. It is more difficult to allow for the distortion in relative prices. It would, however, appear that capital goods, particularly the imported ones, have been underpriced relative to other goods. As the more intensive user of these goods, the large-scale industries would be at an even greater disadvantage if actual scarcity prices were used. Small-scale industries also appear to use some, though less, imported capital goods but they have usually been less successful in directly importing these goods through licensing. The scarcity premium has often been appropriated by the intermediaries.

It would seem reasonable to conclude that small-scale industries make the best use of scarce resources, although this does not indicate that small-scale industries can even incrementally take the place of large-scale ones, because some products can only be produced in large units for technological or efficiency considerations.

A full explanation of the above will not be attempted here. To do so would require the analysis of each technique in great detail, including technological and organisational aspects. We

[1] See A. R. Khan and A. MacEwan, 'A Multisectoral Analysis of Capital Requirements for Development Planning in Pakistan', *The Pakistan Development Review*, winter 1967.

would, however, like to emphasise one aspect of the explanatory factors, relative factor prices. The cost of capital assets for a private investor would be determined by two sets of prices – prices of credit needed to finance investment; and the prices of investment goods. The big industrialists had easy access to cheap credit in an oligopolistic banking system.[1] They also

TABLE 6.2

CAPITAL/VALUE-ADDED RATIOS IN LARGE-SCALE, SMALL-SCALE AND COTTAGE INDUSTRIES

	Large-scale	Small-scale	Cottage
Sugar/Gur*	3·619	0·424	0·776
Edible oil	1·555	0·630	0·630
Cigarette/Bidi*	0·573	0·100	0·100
Other Food, Drink etc.	1·613	0·280	0·465
Cotton textiles	2·751	0·364	0·606
Jute textiles*	2·462	0·104	0·182
Other textiles	7·048	0·358	0·610
Paper/Printing*	13·798	2·074	0·518
Leather and Leather Goods	1·269	0·189	0·520
Rubber Goods	1·851	0·252	—
Fertiliser	12·661	—	—
Chemicals	0·719	0·677	0·608
Cement	2·642	—	—
Basic Metals	1·246	—	—
Metal Products	1·624	0·976	0·107
Machineries	2·002	0·654	0·410
Transport equipment*	1·759	0·482	0·271
Wood, Cork, Furniture	2·437	0·612	0·473
Miscellaneous	2·664	0·501	0·352

* Sectors for which the product composition differs greatly between large-scale and small-scale industry.

SOURCE
A. R. Khan and A. MacEwan, 'A Multisectoral Analysis of Capital Requirements for Development Planning in Pakistan', The *Pakistan Development Review*, winter 1967.

[1] Most of them were West Pakistanis with political influence with the Government.

imported capital goods through licenses at the official rate of exchange, which meant an artificially low price for such goods. In comparison, smaller industrialists had much greater difficulty in obtaining credit. They also had relatively little access to import licenses and were more often forced to buy either from (West Pakistani) manufacturers or through importing middlemen. Thus the price of capital was lower for the bigger industrialists than for the smaller. On the other hand, the price of labour was higher for the bigger industrialists than for the smaller ones. This was partly due to the minimum wage legislation which applied to the former and not to the latter. Also whatever little trade unionism was permitted was concentrated in the bigger enterprises. Finally, the bigger industries wanted to be located in areas already having a high concentration of industry in order to take advantage of facilities and this inevitably drove wages up. The fact that capital was relatively cheaper and labour relatively dearer for the bigger enterprises must explain a good deal of the differential pattern of factor use.

6.3 LARGE-SCALE INDUSTRIES

The large-scale manufacturing industries in Bangladesh consist of about a thousand enterprises each employing, on the average, just over 230 workers.[1] They employ about 1 per cent of the labour force and contribute about 6 per cent of GDP. Many of the larger enterprises were set up or bought by West Pakistani capitalists. Because of the sensitive issues involved, no estimate of the extent of West Pakistani ownership is readily available. Considering that the outstandingly big ones, the Karnaphully paper and rayon mills and the Adamjee jute mills, to name just a few of the giants, have been owned by them and that their ownership is extensive in terms of numbers among the smaller firms as well, it may not be wrong to put it at over half the industrial assets.[2]

[1] The 1967/68 CMI reports 927 2(j) enterprises with an average employment per enterprise of 231.

[2] In an interview with the correspondent of the *Sunday Times*, the Industries Minister of the Government of Bangladesh said that the large-scale enterprises deserted by the (West) Pakistanis after the independence of Bangladesh were 35 per cent of all such enterprises. See *Sunday Times*, 6 Feb. 1972.

It is a small mystery how the West Pakistani capitalists and traders came to own such massive assets in industry and trade. The classic mechanism of such ownership is through foreign investment which would show up as a corresponding trade deficit of the country in which ownership is being taken over and a trade surplus of the country which is taking over ownership. Such ownership in Bangladesh was mainly generated during the fifties and early sixties, a period during which she not only had no deficit in her trade but actually had a surplus. West Pakistan during the same period had a massive deficit in trade, not the kind of circumstance that would allow net investment abroad. It would all appear very puzzling that in spite of all these indications to the contrary, West Pakistan was acquiring large assets in Bangladesh in the decade and a half after the creation of Pakistan.

The mystery will probably never be fully resolved now that the story is buried in the official records of Pakistan's Ministry of Commerce, State Bank and other agencies. The following explanation, however, would appear to go a long way to solve the puzzle.

Soon after the creation of Pakistan, the Government opted for the policy of keeping the external rate of exchange of the rupee over-valued and of rationing import entitlements through licenses. Import licenses meant large income subsidies, as the price of the imported goods in the starved domestic market was way above the c.i.f. price at the official exchange rate plus taxes and 'normal' traders' profit. Although Bangladesh in those years earned up to two-thirds of the exports of the then Pakistan, West Pakistan received 70-odd per cent of imports. The import trade of Bangladesh was also largely in the hands of the West Pakistani traders. Thus against a very high proportion of Bangladesh exports, the earnings of which were compulsorily surrendered at a low rupee price which constituted a high concealed tax, the West Pakistani traders got import licenses. These entitlements allowed them to earn large profits both in the markets of Bangladesh and in West Pakistan. They must have converted some of these into ownership of assets in Bangladesh. Once an initial acquisition was made, later increase in ownership was further facilitated by high profits in the protected market.

A consequence of the emergence of Bangladesh through violent secession is to make the State the immediate owner of the West Pakistani enterprises. Along with the enterprises owned by the Industrial Development Corporation, this would give the State a massive control over manufacturing industries, perhaps including well over two-thirds of the industrial assets and output. This would both be an opportunity and a challenge – an opportunity, in so far as the otherwise modest sources of public sector revenue would be greatly augmented; and a challenge, in so far as the Government with limited managerial resources and meagre experience of running commercial enterprises will be faced with the problem of managing a very large number of units.

The large-scale industries today can by no means be characterised as the result of two decades of dynamic growth. During her political association with Pakistan Bangladesh experienced a fairly mild rate of industrialisation mainly under 'metropolitan' ownership and concentrated in the extraction or processing of indigenous raw materials.

Some of the information about output, employment and value-added in the leading large-scale industries is shown in Tables 6.3 and 6.4.

The thirteen industries listed in the latter table account for 77 per cent of employment and 80 per cent of value-added in large-scale manufacturing. Jute textile is by far the largest of all these industries, employing 47 per cent of all workers employed in large-scale manufacturing. The industry started out with the objective of replacing part of raw jute exports by that of manufactured jute goods. It received extraordinarily preferential treatment in comparison with that meted out to the growers of raw jute. Manufactured jute goods have been exported at a preferential rate of exchange made available though an export bonus. The preferential rate of exchange was not the only incentive given to this industry. To protect it from competitors elsewhere in world trade, it was necessary to keep the world market price of raw jute high and the domestic market price low. This was achieved by exporting raw jute at an artificially overvalued rate of exchange in relation to the domestic currency. It is doubtful whether government policy would have gone to such extraordinary lengths at the cost of the jute growers' real income and the gradual decline in Bangladesh's share in the world jute exports if the industry were not spearheaded by some of the most powerful capitalist families of West Pakistan.[1]

TABLE 6.3

OUTPUT OF SELECTED MANUFACTURING
INDUSTRIES IN BANGLADESH

	1954–55	*1959–60*	*1964–65*	*1968–69*	*1969–70*
Tea (million lbs)	53·8	50·3	62·3	63·7	69·6
Sugar (thousand tons)	47	61	77	57	89
Vegetable oil					
(thousand tons)	—	1·8	4·9	5·7	6·4
Cigarettes (million)	400	1100	5540	16850	17780
Cotton yarn (million lbs)	23	49	64	95	106
Cotton cloth					
(million yards)	64	62	49	61	59
Rayon cloth					
(million yards)	—	0·3	0·1	6·8	5·0
Jute manufactures					
(thousand tons)	103	265	289	518	580
Fertiliser (urea)					
(thousand tons)	—	—	72	87	94
Matches					
(million gross boxes)	2·4	8·6	10·7	13·2	13·0
Cement					
(thousand tons)	50	61	56	63	53
Paper and newsprint					
(thousand tons)	19·2	39·2	78·8	82·7	77·9

SOURCE

Government of Pakistan (Ministry of Finance), *Pakistan Economic Survey 1970–71* (Islamabad, 1971).

By 1970 the industry had an estimated capacity of 22,000 looms. It already had a moderate share of public ownership. With the takeover of the West Pakistani enterprises, the state will control an overwhelming proportion of output capacity.

The industry produces almost entirely for export. During the three years 1964/65 to 1966/67, about 86 per cent of output was exported abroad, excluding West Pakistan. Including exports to West Pakistan, the proportion would be just over 92 per cent.

[1] A detailed discussion of the policies leading to differential incentives for raw and manufactured jute is contained in Chapter 8.

The Bangladesh export of jute textiles during the same period was 24 per cent of the world total and 36 per cent of Indian exports. Together India and Bangladesh accounted for 90 per cent of world exports. Except for capital goods, the industry is not significantly import-dependent; imported raw materials were no more than 3 per cent of the total.[1]

TABLE 6.4

EMPLOYMENT AND VALUE-ADDED IN MAJOR
LARGE-SCALE INDUSTRIES IN BANGLADESH
1967/68

Industry	Employment (number)	Value-added (million Rs.)	Rank in terms of Value-added
1. Jute textile	100,500	299·2	1
2. Cotton textile	33,887	146·7	3
3. Tea processing	9,803	115·9	4
4. Matches	9,101	48·5	7
5. Paper	5,301	51·2	6
6. Cigarettes	3,926	214·1	2
7. Jute baling	3,588	42·6	8
8. Shipbuilding	3,242	11·3	13
9. Perfumes etc.	3,217	39·1	9
10. Drugs and medicines	3,075	32·9	11
11. Iron and steel	1,778	27·8	12
12. Fertiliser	1,527	38·6	10
13. Rayon	357	57·9	5

SOURCE
CMI, 1967/68.

That Bangladesh was able to cut sharply into the Indian share of the export market for jute manufactures should not be taken as an indicator of the real competitiveness of the industry as compared with its Indian counterpart. The Indian jute manufacturing industry not only paid a 50 per cent higher wage and a 25 per cent higher price for raw jute, but also received a far less favourable rate of exchange for its export earnings. Although the official exchange rate of the Indian rupee has been lower than that in Bangladesh (then East Pakistan) since 1966, the effective rate of exchange for Bangladesh exports of jute manufactures (Rs. 9·8 per dollar in recent years, as shown in

[1] According to the CMI, 1965/66.

Chapter 8 below) was far more favourable than that for Indian exports of jute manufactures (no higher than about Rs. 6·5 per dollar in recent years, after allowing for the export tax that was reimposed with the 1966 devaluation). Even neglecting the difference in wages, the absence of free trade in raw jute and the difference in the rates of exchange meant that per dollar worth of jute manufactures export, the Indian manufacturer was being additionally 'taxed' to the extent of roughly Rs. 3·5 as compared with the Bangladesh manufacturers. It is quite certain that it would not be nearly so easy for the largely (West) Pakistani-owned Bangladesh jute manufactures to cut into the Indian share except for the massive differential in incentives. It is ironic that the economic policies of her worst enemy were rein-forcing the policy distortions introduced by the Pakistan Government to achieve an objective especially profitable to the interest of the groups it represented!

While the jute textile industry is export-oriented but based on an indigenous raw material, the next biggest large-scale industry, cotton textiles, is a domestic-consumption-oriented activity based largely on imported raw materials. Given the need to import the raw cotton that was formerly supplied by West Pakistan, the imported inputs are 78 per cent of all current inputs and 44 per cent of the value of output at pro-ducers' prices. We have already indicated that this industry's share of total domestic cotton textiles is only 10 per cent, the other 90 per cent being produced by small-scale and cottage industries. However, there are two important considerations which are likely to ensure some incremental importance to this industry. First, it supplies much of the yarn which determines the level of operation of small and cottage textile enterprises. Second, Bangladesh used to import a large quantity of textile and yarn from West Pakistan and economic calculations indi-cate the desirability of the substitution of these imports (see Chapter 10). To do so, the capacity of the industry will have to be doubled.

Tea, a combination of plantation and manufacturing, was domestically consumed by Bangladesh only to the extent of 18·6 per cent of production during the sixties. Much of the balance used to be exported, mainly to the U.K., which made tea the second most important foreign exchange earner during the fifties. The phenomenal increase in consumption in West Pakistan, combined with the highly unfavourable rate of exchange,[1] gradually converted the entire exports of tea abroad to exports to West Pakistan. Today, after independence, Bangladesh regains the exportable surplus of more than 50 million pounds for which it has to find a share in the world tea export market. In view of the fact that West Pakistan has already entered the world market as a buyer, there should not be too much difficulty in doing so.

Tea plantations and tea processing had a rather high concentration of external ownership, both British and West Pakistani. They also have about the lowest wage rate of all employment categories and a very high market rate of return. And yet there has been too little investment in the past. As a consequence the rate of growth in output has been very low, only about 1·7 per cent per year during the decade and a half leading to 1970.

Paper, an extraordinarily capital-intensive industry, has grown as an import substitute and regional export to West Pakistan. Starting with the huge public sector paper mill at Karnaphully (later transferred to West Pakistani private ownership), the industry kept growing through the setting up of newsprint factories in Khulna and, in very recent years, an additional paper mill in North Bengal. The justification of this highly capital-intensive industry as an enterprise using indigenous raw materials does not appear wholly convincing since 45 per cent of all raw materials were imported from abroad.[2] Once again, the independence of Bangladesh has meant a substantial export surplus valued at around 110 million rupees.

Cigarettes, matches, sugar and rayon textiles are some of the other important consumption goods industries. Among these, matches were also exported to West Pakistan. Besides, there is some domestic capacity in edible oils, chemicals of various kinds, leather and rubber goods for domestic consumption.

[1] Tea was not eligible for export bonus, so that a dollar from its export continued to be exchanged for Rs. 4·75 while a dollar from typical manufactured exports and some agricultural exports (like fine rice) was being exchanged for Rs. 7·60 or more (a 40 per cent export bonus and a premium of a minimum of 150 per cent on a bonus voucher). Even then tea exports had to be banned to encourage consumption domestically, mainly in West Pakistan, for a period in the early sixties.

[2] According to the CMI, 1965/66.

Very few capital goods or materials for capital goods are domestically produced. The only steel mill, going into production in 1967 at Chittagong, has a small capacity of 150,000 tons and was recently being expanded by another 100,000 tons. Cement production, long stagnant at a fraction of domestic requirement, was being planned for some expansion on the basis of imported clinker. The machinery industry was to get a big boost through the Machine Tools Project near Dacca, scheduled to be completed by 1972; by 1970, it had already started assembling important components.

Even at the extremely low level of its use, fertiliser is only fractionally supplied by domestic production, which until recently was entirely in the form of urea. A large expansion was to be achieved by the early seventies with the incremental share of urea well below half.

The large-scale industries of Bangladesh were provided with quite a high proportion of public sector ownership. The Industrial Development Corporation set up a large number of enterprises and pioneered in most new areas. During the five-year period ending in 1970, its share in total industrial investment was over half. Over the years, however, the Industrial Development Corporation had divested itself of many of the going projects on the principle that once an enterprise becomes viable (i.e. begins yielding profits) its ownership should be transferred to private capitalists and that resources obtained through sales should be used to finance new ventures. Since the indigenous capitalists in Bangladesh were no match for their West Pakistani counterparts in terms of command over resources and credit-worthiness, much of the ownership of the Bangladesh industries, nurtured by public resources during their infancy, were transferred to West Pakistani capitalists. However, there seems to have been little substance in the argument of raising additional resources through sales. The private buyers financed their purchases not by their accumulated savings but by cheap bank credit to which they had access in an oligopolistic banking system. It is amazing that such credit was not made available directly to the public sector Industrial Development Corporation.

6.4 THE EFFICIENCY OF INDUSTRIES: EFFECTIVE
PROTECTION AND SOCIAL RATE OF RETURN

In recent years a good deal of discussion has been going on
about the efficiency of the industrialisation programmes promoted through high and non-uniform protection. The argument runs as follows: in most of the developing countries
embarking on industrialisation programmes, imports are
quantitatively restricted. The resulting structure of prices
becomes highly arbitrary without any correspondence to social
scarcities or scarcities in the world market. The contribution to
national output by any industry at these distorted prices would
be a misleading indicator of the sector's real contribution.

Much of the quantification of the phenomenon has been
carried out in terms of measuring the effective rate of protection, defined as the ratio of value-added at market prices to
value-added at world prices (i.e. the prices that would obtain
under free trade). Effective protection measures the proportion
of value-added that is due to the distortions in relative prices
separately from the ones that would result under free trade.
Compared to the free-trade situation it therefore measures the
additional payment that can be made to the primary factors of
production, capital and labour. If industries differ with respect
to effective protection, it would appear that their capacities to
bid away resources in excess of what they would be able to do
under free trade would differ. This would result in a misallocation of resources to the corresponding extent.[1]

Such measurements have been made for a number of developing countries. Unfortunately no estimate for Bangladesh industries is available, although they have been prepared for the
industries in former Pakistan, of which Bangladesh was then a
part.[2]

We shall describe briefly the results of an exercise carried out
by us to analyse the efficiency of industries in Bangladesh. The

[1] For a discussion of the theory of effective protection see W. M. Corden,
The Theory of Protection, (Oxford University Press, 1971). Measurements of
effective protection have been reported in Little, I. M. D., T. Scitovsky and
M. FG. Scott, *Industry and Trade* (Oxford University Press, 1970).
[2] This has been done by Stephen Lewis Jr and Stephen Guisinger and
reported in Little, Scitovsky and Scott, op. cit.

exercise is based on the application of the results of a 'model of accounting prices' developed jointly by Professor J. A. Mirrlees and the present writer.[1] While effective protection measurements take the free trade solution as the optimal situation, our method is based on measuring accounting prices as indicators of social scarcities under a somewhat different definition of the optimal situation. In Chapter 10 we shall provide an outline of the method of obtaining the accounting prices of the various individual products simultaneously by using a multisectoral model.

Table 6.5 shows the market rates of return, the social rates of return (i.e. the rates of return on the assumption that all transactions were made at the accounting prices reflecting true social scarcities) and the ratios of value-added at market prices to that at accounting prices (showing the additional command of the relevant industry over primary resources due to the distortion in the arbitrary market prices) for 19 tradeable industry groups.

Since the purpose of the exercise was to ascertain the priority of investment allocation, the production structure of each sector was based on the part that could be expected to grow fast, the large-scale industries. Cotton textiles, metal products and miscellaneous manufactures are the only sectors for which some weight was accorded to small-scale industry. The basic data were obtained from the 1962/63 CMI although some of the findings of the later CMIs were incorporated to take major changes into account. Thus the results of the table mainly describe the efficiency of the large-scale industries of Bangladesh during the sixties.

In general, the social profitability of these industries is much less than private profitability, but the gap between the two differs widely from one industry to another.

Also a very high proportion of value-added in these industries is due to the distortions in relative prices, meaning that if all inputs and outputs were evaluated at accounting prices (i.e. relative social scarcities), value-added in many industries would be less than half. Sugar and cigarettes have negative social profits though fairly high private ones; their production seems to result in a net reduction in society's real income. Paper too

[1] The model and its results are as yet unpublished, but an account in outline is provided in Chapter 10 of the present study.

has a negative social return, which is not surprising in view of its extraordinarily high capital intensity in an economy in which the scarcity of capital is reflected in the high accounting cost of its use.

TABLE 6.5

DIFFERENTIAL INCENTIVES AND EFFICIENCY

Industry Group	Market Rate of Return (%)	Social Rate of Return (%)	Value-added at Market Price ÷ VA at Accounting Price
Tea	25·05	15·89	1·69
Sugar	13·05	−7·38	Negative*
Edible oils	39·07	15·82	2·53
Cigarettes	54·01	−38·52	Negative*
Miscellaneous food	74·25	15·81	2·95
Cotton textile	19·83	15·87	1·62
Jute textile	24·78	15·89	2·05
Other textile	12·38	−1·52	2·27
Paper	4·41	−0·41	4·79
Leather and leather goods	62·75	15·72	2·34
Rubber goods	21·80	2·24	3·13
Fertiliser	6·61	10·65	0·92
Chemicals	54·65	15·86	2·80
Cement	7·55	6·78	1·54
Basic metals	25·73	15·89	2·04
Metal products	20·22	15·86	2·12
Machinery	14·95	15·89	2·29
Transport equipment	22·18	15·87	1·94
Miscellaneous Manufactures	16·43	7·25	1·84

* Value-added at accounting prices is negative.

The industries were clearly made privately highly profitable, though their social profitability was fairly low for most sectors and too low for some sectors to justify the past expansion. One notable exception is fertiliser, for which the private profit rate was lower than the social rate of return. For almost all other sectors, the artificial distortions in market incentives, brought about by direct controls imposed on trade and economic activities, have made investment artificially and arbitrarily attractive. What is more is that such differentials between market and social rates of return have varied between industries. The real income and consumption of the society have been considerably less as a consequence of the allocation of resources guided by these distorted incentives than they would have been if the incentives had been consistent with social scarcities.

The last column of Table 6.5 shows that the value-added by manufacturing at market prices would be a highly exaggerated indicator of the sector's true contribution to real GDP. In fact, value-added in manufacturing at accounting prices is only 45 per cent of that at market prices; and since the real value-added in non-manufacturing sectors is also below the market value (though to a lesser extent), the real share of manufacturing in real GDP would be 16 per cent less (i.e. its share at real value is about 5 per cent of real GDP if its market value is about 6 per cent of GDP at market prices).

The results quoted above cast serious doubt on the efficiency and real utility of the large-scale manufacturing industry set up in the past in Bangladesh. We could not do a similar analysis of the small-scale and cottage enterprises for want of detailed information about their input structures, but there is little doubt that they would come out much better. As we shall see later, much of the high accounting price is explained by the high social cost of using large quantities of capital. Since the small-scale and cottage enterprises use a tiny fraction of the amounts of capital used by the large-scale industries, their accounting costs of production would be far more favourable.

7 Economic Overheads

7.1 ABSENCE OF 'FORWARD LINKAGE'

ECONOMIC overheads like power, transport and communications are important sources of so-called 'forward linkages'. If their supplies are elastic, industrial, agricultural and other types of economic activity are provided with external economies. If, however, their supplies are inelastic at the margin, the profitability of the using industries tends to be low and economic growth faces bottlenecks. Whatever may be the appeal of some models of unbalanced growth which tend to attribute little usefulness to the provision of forward linkages alone, it is difficult to imagine continued industrial and agricultural growth with the investors always worrying about the ability of the overhead facilities to bear the additional burden.

More than any other sector of the economy, the economic overheads in Bangladesh would appear to be inadequate and overstretched. It has been impossible in the past not to expand the facilities at all, but all 'expensive' programmes have been successfully postponed by the rulers and planners in Islamabad. As a consequence, independent Bangladesh today inherits an over-used and inadequate infrastructure with marks of patchwork all over it.

7.2 POWER

Power supply is an important bottleneck for the Bangladesh economy. Over the years, expensive electric power has not only been one of the minor causes of the relatively high cost of manufacturing, but its uncertain supply has often been a major cause of the under-utilisation of capacity. To insure against such uncertainty, many manufacturing units have set up their own generating plants, thereby raising the capital cost both because of the higher capital cost in electricity generation than in manufacturing industries and because of the uneconomic size and/or excess capacity in these industrial power generating plants. As is shown in Table 7.1, *per capita* generating capacity in Bangladesh in recent times at ·007 kW has been one of the lowest in the world; it is about a quarter of that in India and just over a fifth of that in (West) Pakistan.

The relative price of electricity has been higher in Bangladesh than in her subcontinental neighbours. And yet it appears that given the existing structure of its production, electricity is underpriced in the sense that it does not cover its social cost of production![1] It is, however, not quite necessary to conclude that power is inevitably socially expensive to the extent indicated. During the phase of laying the national grid with a small generating base, the capital cost of transmission becomes disproportionately high. Also some indication is available that much of the high cost in the past was due to the uneconomic size of plants.

The country has very little unexploited hydro-electric potential. Thus the choice has to be among the various fuel-based thermal power generation methods. Here, the circumstances were somewhat changed in recent years owing to the discovery of gas reserves.[2] Also, the opening of trade with India makes it possible to import coal at much lower cost than before, thereby increasing the attractiveness of this conventional fuel. Finally, in recent years a great deal of speculation has been going on about the economic sense of a nuclear plant. In fact, the procrastination of the then Pakistan Government with the blueprint for a nuclear plant at Ruppur made the demand for it one of the focal points of the nationalist upsurge in Bengal. Today it appears to be of very great priority that a careful analysis of the social benefits and costs of the alternative methods of power generation be carried out.

[1] This is based on the Model of Accounting Prices developed by the present author and Professor J. A. Mirrlees. An exposition of the model is given in Chapter 10. The accounting price of electricity appears to be about 65 per cent higher than the market price. For almost every other product, the accounting price is below the market price.

[2] No definitive estimate of the reserves is available, but very conservative geological measurements claim the known reserves to be 9·3 thousand billion cubic feet (see the *Fourth Five-Year Plan*, p. 409). At the current rate of use in *Pakistan* (where it is many times higher than in Bangladesh) the known reserves alone would last for 150 years!

Power supply today is entirely limited to the few urban areas and industrial units. The villages where 93 per cent of the people live are by and large without any electricity. There is little doubt that there will be no significant demand if individual rural households are to be charged the average cost of generation and transmission. It is, however, an important question to be studied whether, in view of the supposed 'external economies' of electric power and its crucial role in making possible some kind of decentralised, socially desirable, labour-using industrialisation, it is worth while to ignore the dictates of the market and the existing income distribution in taking it to where the nation lives.

7.3 TRANSPORT

One of the few advantages of having a great many people living in a small area is the low *per capita* social capital requirement in the form of roads and railway lines (and also power transmission lines), although the requirement of such capital *per square mile* would be higher than if population density were much less. In Bangladesh the combined railway and metalled road mileage of 0·76 per square mile of area would nevertheless appear to be too low a level.

A look at Table 7.1 would show that railways have been absolutely stagnant. With initial facilities extremely meagre, there has been a 10 per cent increase in route mileage (and a lower increase in track mileage which is not shown in the table) in nearly two-and-a-half decades. Rolling stock, on the average has increased at no greater rate. It is somewhat surprising that over the fifteen years ending in 1970 passenger mileage increased by three-quarters and cargo ton-mileage nearly doubled with locomotives increasing only 4 per cent, coaches less than 9 per cent and wagons less than 24 per cent. It would be madness to argue that this is because of excess capacity in the mid-fifties, for anyone who cares to remember would know that the facilities were overcrowded then.

Nor does it make sense to talk about the capacity utilisation of any particular kind of capital in such a network of a system. Thus track may remain under-utilised while rolling stock is more than fully utilised because of the inappropriate proportion between them. More intriguingly, a single-track route may be able to handle only a third as much traffic, or less, as a double-track route because a good deal of idleness of track is technologically enforced by the need to handle traffic both ways. Thus the only way to increase capacity utilisation in rolling stock *and tracks* may be to create more capacity in tracks!

In Bangladesh it would appear that the system is being utilised at more than optimum capacity in the sense of causing a good deal of delay in commodity and personnel movement, thereby raising the working capital needs of the whole economy. Even the crucially important lines between the ports and major urban centres are single-tracked, causing extremely slow movement. Not only is the system absolutely incapable of coping with the mildest of emergencies, but is also highly inefficient in normal activities.

TABLE 7.1

ECONOMIC OVERHEADS

Power	*1965*	*1969*	*1970*		
Generation (Th.kW)	300	363	488		
Transmission lines (miles)	—	5322	5697		

Power generating capacity in kW per thousand people:
   India (1968) = 27
   West Pakistan (now Pakistan) (1970) = 32
   Bangladesh (1970) = 7

Road Transport	*1960*	*1965*	*1970*		
Metalled roads (miles)*	995	1964	2398		
Number of buses and trucks	5564	10134	14386 (*1969*)		

Railway	*1948*	*1955*	*1960*	*1965*	*1970*
Route mileage*	1619	1708	1714	1713	1776
Locomotives	—	464	472	486	484
Coaches	—	1538	1621	1790	1674
Wagons	—	15965	15860	19509	19756
Million passenger miles†	—	1373	1816	1922	2425
Million cargo ton-miles†	—	472	872	893	921

* Metalled road and railway route mileage together per square mile of territory in 1970 = 0·76.

† Fiscal year ending June of each year.

SOURCE

Ministry of Finance (Islamabad), *Pakistan Economic Survey 1970–71*; Planning Department (Dacca), *East Pakistan Economic Survey 1969–70*; C.S.O., *Statistical Yearbook 1968*.

Road transport would appear to have expanded much faster than railways though the aggregate of road and railway facilities together are still dismally inadequate. It also appears that a decision had been made to provide the entire incremental transport route in the form of roads, keeping the railway routes pretty much unchanged. Whether this has been the right decision cannot be said without a proper analysis of the social benefits and costs for each. Such a comparison will require a great deal of detailed information about the input structure in each and the substitution of distorted market prices by appropriate scarcity prices. Since it is neither our intention nor a particularly feasible task to enter into such an exercise at this stage of our present work, we shall merely confine ourselves to a few generalities. The option for the roads seems no doubt to have been dictated by its lower capital cost at market prices. Even without going into the question of whether such costs are at all appropriate measures of the *social* values of capital committed, we might point out that the operating costs are estimated to be more than twice as high for roads. Thus while the cost per ton-mile on railways varies between Rs. 0·21 and Rs. 0·24, that for road for the corresponding routes varies between Rs. 0·53 and Rs. 0·83.[1] No estimate of the difference in capital cost is available but it is believed to be proportionately much less.

It has been argued, though little actual information has been provided, that inland waterways should be an even cheaper means of transport in riverine Bangladesh.[2] Consequently, some investment had been undertaken by the Inland Water Transport Authority in the late sixties by developing five inland river ports (at Dacca, Narayanganj, Chandpur, Barisal and Khulna) and acquiring and operating a number of mechanical crafts. Also the (then East Pakistan) Shipping Corporation, set up in 1964, had by 1970 been operating four coastal ships between the capital city and the main port at Chittagong via the offshore islands. While such bits of transport facilities have been of use to industry and trade growing slowly, it seems inevitable that a big investment in these services will

[1] See Planning Commission, *Report of the Advisory Panel on Inland Water Transport of East Pakistan* (Islamabad, July 1970).
[2] See ibid. for some rudimentary estimates.

have to be undertaken when economic activity experiences a discontinuous jump.

Since independence, the inadequacy of the transport system has been a much greater bottleneck than before. The effect of the 1971 war has been most severe in this sector. An estimated three hundred bridges of various sizes were damaged. Nearly 240 of them have been temporarily repaired within weeks of independence, according to an estimate of the Ministry of Rehabilitation made in late February 1972. The speed with which the economy can be restored to its pre-war level would very much depend on the pace at which these facilities are put back to a working condition.

7.4 HARNESSING THE RIVERS

In our discussion of agriculture, we referred to the problem of flooding. Excessive flooding has been a major source of uncertainty to agriculture in Bangladesh. Almost the whole of Bangladesh lies in the delta of three mighty rivers, the Padma (the local name of the Ganges), the Jamuna (the local name of the Brahmaputra) and the Meghna. The three rivers are estimated to drain an approximate area of 0·6 million square miles, only about 8 per cent of which lies in Bangladesh. Thus the control of flooding can hardly be attempted without the co-operation of the upstream riparian countries, mainly India. This is particularly so in view of the absence of any storage site within Bangladesh that could assist in flood regulation and the likelihood that such a site may exist in the upstream riparian countries. The enormity of the technical problem involved is suggested by the magnitude of the peak flood flow (five million cusecs or twice the all-time peak flood of the Mississippi River) and the sediment load (about 2·4 billion tons a year for the three rivers together) which is greater than that of any other river system in the world.

From eight to ten million acres of cultivable land on the average are flooded annually by spills from the main rivers and by local run-off from the heavy monsoons. Some flooding is caused by the tributaries draining hilly areas in Indo-Bangladesh border. About three million acres are subject to flooding with varying degrees of salinity due to oceanic tides and typhoonic tidal waves. Over fifteen million acres, or two-thirds of the cultivated land, are subject from time to time to one or other kind of flooding, although for any single year the total area has been rather less.

About the direct damage caused by flooding there are only rudimentary estimates available. In 1962 the amount of rice lost due to flooding is estimated to have been 1·2 million tons, valued then at 220 million dollars.[1] The loss in 1968, not quantified by a distant Government which did not even try to do so and did everything to avoid committing itself to a pro-gramme of flood control, is believed to have been higher. There have of course been other losses in terms of death to cattle, destruction of houses and assets and damage to the transporta-tion system.

The fact that the probability of flooding looms large in the expectation of the farmer changes his whole decision process. In deeply flooded lands (e.g. over fifteen feet in the Meghna valley) there is little incentive for cultivation at all if the farmer knows from experience that in two out of three years flooding is to be expected. With this kind of probability distribution and the known output per acre of twelve maunds, the average expectation of the farmer is as low as four maunds per acre. This hardly justifies any effort beyond what is otherwise wasted anyway. In lands that are flooded from three to twelve feet, the farmers can only grow low-yielding Aus and transplanted Aman, subject of course to the usual risk which reduces the expectation of yield and thereby the incentive to invest. This also limits the possibility of using fertiliser, improved seed and modern technology in general.

In the past, the problem of flood control was entirely side-tracked, with the consequence that our knowledge of the tech-nical alternatives for a solution is nearly non-existent. For a time, it was perhaps even hoped, at least implicitly, that by increasing winter acreage the problem of controlling flood could be shelved for a long time. In the long-term perspective, such an attitude would appear to be dangerously naïve. In the absence of a hydrological survey, it is hardly possible to estimate

[1] I.B.R.D., *Proposals for An Action Program: East Pakistan Agriculture and Water Department*, 17 July 1970, The statistics quoted above are mainly from this source.

how far one could go by way of increasing winter acreage. Even with fairly optimistic assumptions, it would be impossible to make any drastic reduction in the dependence on rainy season crops. The technical advance of rainy season agriculture is, as we have shown above, directly dependent on the ability to reduce the risk of flooding.

8 External Trade and Self-Reliance

8.1 REGIONAL TRADE WITH PAKISTAN AND THE CONSEQUENCES OF ITS CESSATION

THE central fact about the economy of Bangladesh over the last quarter-century was its membership in a fully integrated customs union with Pakistan (then West Pakistan) with an exceedingly high (effective) common external tariff which had assymetrical effects on the trade patterns of the two members of the union. Almost the entire import into Bangladesh from Pakistan was trade diversion in the sense that except for the common external tariff these goods would be imported from elsewhere. On the other hand, Pakistan's imports from Bangladesh did not replace cheaper imports into the former. These were the goods that Bangladesh exported elsewhere as well. The essential fact of the customs union was the arbitrariness and non-uniformity of the tariff structure determined by the multiple weapons of control operated by a Government located in and representing the interests of trade and industry in what was then West Pakistan. The whole pattern of inter-regional trade evolved a mechanism of resource transfer which has been briefly analysed in earlier chapters.

The main elements of the mechanism can be described as below: (*a*) by erecting a generally very high effective common external tariff and by direct control of import entitlement, a large import flow from relatively more industrialised West Pakistan into Bangladesh was created; (*b*) this was only partly offset by Bangladesh exports to West Pakistan, the other part being converted into foreign exchange resources of Bangladesh (its export surplus until the early sixties and its foreign aid share in recent years) at the officially overvalued rate of exchange of the domestic currency; (*c*) systematic discriminations in the exchange rate were made to keep West Pakistan's non-competitive imports from Bangladesh cheap. Thus tea, formerly the second biggest export of Bangladesh abroad, was entirely redirected into exports to West Pakistan by keeping its effective rate of exchange in export one of the most unfavourable. Similarly paper, another important export of Bangladesh to West Pakistan, was kept cheap by keeping its exchange rate in possible exports at the unfavourable official rate while exports in general qualified for much more favourable effective rates.

As a consequence of the independence of Bangladesh, no significant portion of imports from West Pakistan is likely to survive even if political relations were, by some miracle, to be normalised. These will be replaced by cheaper imports from elsewhere or, in the longer run, by domestic production. On the other hand, Bangladesh exports to West Pakistan should be able to find alternative markets. They used to be, and often still are, exported elsewhere. The additional absorption in the world market should not create a sudden glut in view of the certainty that Pakistan will have to enter as a net buyer.

The pattern of regional trade between Bangladesh and Pakistan is summarised in Table 8.1. The most important of Bangladesh imports have been cotton yarn and textiles. Even in the past, this industry in Bangladesh appeared to have been *socially* more efficient than in West Pakistan.[1] The concentration of investment in the West was due partly to the distortion in the market incentives and partly to the immobility of capital between what were then two wings of Pakistan. There is little doubt that this industry will be a major area of import substitution for the future industrialisation programme of Bangladesh, although in the near future cheaper imports may be obtained, perhaps from India.

The next two important imports of Bangladesh from Pakistan were rice and oilseeds, which could be the targets of a major import substitution programme. No economic sense can be made out of the continued import of rice and almost the first test of the economic success of Bangladesh would be the rapidity with which she attains self-sufficiency in it. Cotton, the next important import, will have to continue to be bought from

[1] This comment is based on the findings of partial studies like A. R. Khan and A. MacEwan, 'A Multisectoral Analysis of Capital Requirement', *The Pakistan Development Review*, winter 1967, and of the more comprehensive study reported below in Chapter 10.

TABLE 8.1

TRADE BETWEEN BANGLADESH AND (WEST) PAKISTAN

(million rupees)

| | Bangladesh Imports | | | | | | Bangladesh Exports | | | |
	Rice and wheat	Cotton textile	Oilseeds	Raw cotton	Tobacco products	Total	Tea	Jute textiles	Paper	Total
1964/65	19·5	254·3	80·4	81·3	89·5	874·5	185·4	104·9	85·9	537·1
1965/66	150·0	285·4	135·6	136·4	103·7	1208·6	243·5	137·5	78·9	651·8
1966/67	150·1	277·9	89·8	93·8	121·5	1324·8	287·3	137·7	76·3	738·9
1967/68	89·7	245·6	114·7	121·0	100·7	1233·2	228·9	140·2	91·0	784·9
1968/69	129·2	278·3	108·8	157·8	123·6	1385·3	257·0	123·8	109·5	870·0

SOURCE
Planning Department, *Economic Survey of East Pakistan 1969–70* (Dacca, 1970).

abroad though the source of supply will have to change. No serious upset is likely since the total Bangladesh requirement is low; the peak annual demand in the past was less than 60,000 tons, i.e. less than 5 per cent of recent Indian production. Cigarettes and drugs and medicines were the next important imports, followed by a large number of consumption goods each quantitatively small.

In contrast, Bangladesh exports to Pakistan were concentrated in fewer goods. Tea, jute manufactures and paper accounted for well over two-thirds of the value. Tea was traditionally exported abroad, mainly to the U.K., reaching a peak of Rs. 56 million in the mid-fifties; it was converted into a regional export through a combination of an unfavourable export exchange rate and direct restrictions. Although the world export market can hardly accept a net addition to supply without a serious price repercussion, Bangladesh should be able to get back much of its export market since West Pakistan will certainly enter the world market as a buyer. In fact, she has already done so. It is doubtful how far she can reduce her purchase in view of the very low price elasticity of tea in the domestic market. No significant reduction in the absorption of this 'mass drink' will be possible without a serious rise in the domestic price, causing considerable consumer unrest. Jute manufactures exported to West Pakistan were a very small proportion of total Bangladesh exports and will be easily exported abroad. In view of India's big paper import and her emergence as a big supplier of imports to Bangladesh, it should not be difficult for Bangladesh to find an outlet for a relatively small quantity of export surplus of paper. Of the next two important exports to Pakistan, leather and matches, there should be no problem in finding an export market for the former although the prospects for the latter are less certain in near future.

An attempt at estimating the net effect of the cessation of trade between Bangladesh and Pakistan may now be made on the assumption that Bangladesh would have to buy all the imports at c.i.f. world prices and sell all the exports at f.o.b. world prices. Very rough calculations show that thus measured the *annual* average of Bangladesh deficit in trade with Pakistan during the last three years shown in Table 8.1 would be about

Rs. 320 million instead of Rs. 517 million actually obtaining in the protected market.

8.2 TRADE WITH THE REST OF THE WORLD: EXPORT AND EXPORT POLICIES

Table 8.2 summarises some of the features of the foreign trade of Bangladesh during the last decade. The most outstanding feature is the complete dominance by jute in raw and processed form; jute accounts for 90 per cent or more of the value of exports abroad. One could possibly argue that this is somewhat deceptive in so far as tea used to be exported in the past and may very likely be resumed as an export. Also some of the other inter-regionally traded goods should perhaps be properly treated as potential exports in so far as they could be sold abroad at a reasonable rate of exchange. But even after all these allowances and adjustments, the dependence on jute in raw and manufactured form seems to be near total.

Another feature of the composition of exports is the steady increase in the share of jute textiles and a decline in the share of raw jute. The way this has been brought about is a classic example of using fiscal policy to effect a transfer of income from the poorer farmers to richer capitalists and from the poorer region to the richer region. What is more, this was done by exposing the sole export of Bangladesh to great uncertainty. It was also a case of technical economists unwittingly playing into the hands of the policymaker to justify the kind of policy whose end they professed to oppose. Let us substantiate each of the statements.[1]

Until 1966–7 raw jute export was subject to an export tax. The foreign exchange earned by raw jute exports had to be surrendered at the official rate of exchange. Thus the effective rate of exchange for raw jute exports (e_r) would be

$$e_r = (1-t)r$$

[1] An excellent reference to the documentation of the above assertions is by Robert Repetto, 'Optimal Export Taxes in the Short and Long Run: Pakistan's Policies Toward Raw Jute Exports', a paper presented at the Dubrovnik conference of the Harvard Development Advisory Service, June 1970. Our discussion in the following paragraphs makes extensive use of his data and arguments although he bears no responsibility for the form in which they are presented.

where $t = $ *ad valorem* rate of export tax[1]

   $r = $ number of rupees exchanging for a dollar at the official rate.

Jute manufactures, on the other hand, have been receiving export bonus since 1959. The scheme operates as follows: a certain proportion (b) of the value of exports is given to the exporter in the form of import entitlements called bonus vouchers. These vouchers are freely marketable and command a price which is some multiple (p) of the face value of the entitlement. Thus the exchange rate for a bonus earning export would be

$$(1+pb)r.$$

To measure the rate of exchange of value added in manufacturing, allowance must be made for the fact that the raw material component of jute textiles (q times the value of manufactured jute) would exchange at the rate $(1-t)r$. Thus the effective rate of exchange for manufactured jute exports (e_m) would be

$$e_m = \frac{(1+pb) - q(1-t)}{1-q} \; r$$

The differential in the incentive to export (which for all practical purposes was equivalent to the differential incentive to produce) may be expressed in terms of an implicit tax on raw jute (T) at the rate

$$T = \frac{e_m - e_r}{e_m}$$

Robert Repetto calculated e_m, e_r and T on the assumption of $q = 0.5$ (which is quite a good approximation) and the actual values of r, t, b and p to get the following measures.[2]

Year	Effective Rate of Exchange: Raw Jute (Rs:$)	Effective Rate of Exchange: Manufactured Jute (Rs:$)	Implicit 'Tax' on Raw Jute
1959/60	4·14	6·86	40%
1962/63	4·24	7·20	41%
1965/66	4·52	6·64	32%
1968/69	4·75	9·84	52%

[1] Export tax was fixed per bale, but can be converted into t by dividing by the unit price of export for any given period.   [2] See Repetto, op. cit.

Thus using jute manufactures as a standard of reference, the disincentive for raw jute can be compared to a 52 per cent tax in recent years!

One may want to be reminded that in the earlier chapter on industries we found that the market rate of return for jute manufactures was much higher than the social rate of return. As we shall show in a later chapter, the market rate of return on raw jute was less than half of the social rate!

What were the reasons behind such a policy? Would it be impossible to develop a jute manufacturing industry without differential protection? Our calculations, reported partly in Chapter 6 and more fully in Chapter 10, show that the social rate of return was high enough for jute textiles to make their domestic production worth while and that it was quite un-necessary to distort the incentive structure to create for them an artificially high rate of profit.

TABLE 8.2

TRADE BETWEEN BANGLADESH AND THE REST OF THE WORLD EXCEPT PAKISTAN

	Exports (million rupees)			Imports
	Raw jute	Jute textiles	Total	Total
1960/61	849·0	310·8	1259·1	1014·4
1961/62	849·8	318·8	1300·6	872·8
1964/65	845·4	292·9	1268·2	1701·8
1965/66	863·1	565·3	1514·1	1328·1
1967/68	758·9	605·5	1484·2	1327·5
1968/69	730·7	655·9	1542·7	1850·0
1969/70	765·6	784·0	1670·1	1813·1

The ostensible justification provided by the official planners (whisperingly rather than clearly, perhaps because they were aware of the true motives) was that the world demand for raw jute was inelastic while that for manufactured jute was not. As Repetto has painstakingly pointed out, the observed low elasticity in some econometric studies has been largely due to the postulation of a demand function which makes quantity purchased in a year the function of price in the *same* year while in reality the effect of a price change takes place over the longer run after there has been enough time for re-equipment or conversion. Also the issue under examination is what demand would be generated if a long period of sustained price reduction were to be assured through the provision of a more favourable rate of exchange for raw jute. It is quite impossible to arrive at any judgement on such a question from the estimation of the demand function from short-term fluctuations of price while the buyers had no anticipation of a long-term sustained reduction in prices.

The share of Bangladesh in world production of jute and allied fibres has declined from 65 per cent during 1947–51 to 32 per cent during 1963–7. Her share in world exports has steadily declined from virtual monopoly in the earlier period to less than half. The foreign demand for Bangladesh jute would depend on (*a*) her market share and (*b*) the supply elasticity in competing producing countries, given the elasticity of world demand. If (*a*) is low and (*b*) is high, the elasticity of demand for Bangladesh jute can still be high in spite of a low elasticity of world demand for all jute exports.[1] An approximation for (*b*) can be made on the basis of the observed supply elasticity in the biggest competitor, Thailand. Elasticity of acreage in the production period immediately following the one in which price is changed has been estimated for Thai Kenaf (a close jute substitute) to be about 2·5.[2] The long-term supply elasticity is found to be greater, in the region of 3·6 to 5·8, depending on the length of the assumed lag and the time period for which the estimate is made.

However, even if we accept the low world demand elasticities for jute measured from the instantaneous demand functions, the elasticity of demand for Bangladesh exports of raw jute would be much higher simply because her share has fallen below 0·5 and the supply elasticity is high for competitors.[3] But the long-

---

[1] The formula used is as follows:

$$e = e_w \, (s/x) - e_s (s - x)/x$$

where e = elasticity of world demand for Bangladesh jute, e_w = elasticity of world demand for all jute and allied fibres, e_s = elasticity of supply of competitors, s = total world export and x = export by Bangladesh. Note that e has the usual negative sign.   [2] See Repetto, op. cit.

[3] Thus e will be $-1·50$ if e_s is assumed to be the lowest of all available estimates (2·5) given the Bangladesh share of 0·5 in world exports and $e_w = -0·50$

term world elasticity for all jute itself is likely to be elastic if its price is kept sufficiently low in the export market and adjustments and re-equipment are allowed to take place. The argument of inelasticity should have no appeal to any but the most naïve of analysts.

Why then was such a policy adopted? In the opinion of the present writer the explanation lies in the fact that jute manufactures were largely owned by politically powerful and wealthy (West Pakistani) capitalists while raw jute was grown by powerless Bengali peasants, the overwhelming proportion of whom were very poor (owning less than a few acres). To maximise their gain from manufacturing, the politically powerful capitalists were not satisfied merely with a reasonable rate of exchange for their exports (through obtaining a bonus on exports at the maximum permissible rate) but also made the Government adopt fiscal measures to drive a wedge between the raw jute price in the domestic market and the world market so that they could have adequate protection against manufacturers abroad. The whole burden, of course, fell on the poor jute growers of Bangladesh. The policies also succeeded in producing a sharp reduction of the Bangladesh share in world exports and thereby threatening this lifeline of Bangladesh with dangerous competition from synthetic fibres which can easily be irreversible in the short and intermediate runs. The policy begun with the cutting off of the Indian market and forcing India into import substitution was systematically carried to the end by the (West) Pakistani authorities through the maximum use of short-term monopoly power to generate enough foreign exchange to finance their needs of industrialisation.

The discussion on exports can be concluded by noting that in the quarter-century during which her partner in the customs union attained significant diversification and an increase in exports, Bangladesh failed to achieve any diversification at all. Almost no significant new export has been added. In fact, exports abroad became more undiversified as a consequence of forcible diversion of some former exports to satisfy the partner region's consumption demand. In a real sense too exports have been stagnant. The value of exports at international purchasing power (i.e. income terms of trade) was less in recent years than in the early fifties.

8.3 IMPORTS FROM ABROAD AND THE DEGREE OF
    SELF-RELIANCE

Till the early sixties Bangladesh had been able to achieve a
significant export surplus in her trade with the outside world.
Since then the surplus has been small and in four years (1963/64,
1964/65, 1968/69 and 1969/70) she had a small deficit. Thus in
fact she had very little *direct* capital inflow from the outside
world even in recent years. The annual average during the
recent five years (1964/65 to 1968/69) was Rs. 78 million. The
remainder of the capital inflow was channelled via (West)
Pakistan, which appropriated the foriegn exchange and paid
Bangladesh in the form of imports from Pakistan in the highly
protected regional trade market. The real value of this capital
inflow in terms of foreign exchange was no more than around
Rs. 268 million on the average during the five-year period under
review.[1] Thus the annual average capital inflow *at its peak* was
no more than Rs. 346 million or about $1 per capita. During the
same period Pakistan received a per capita inflow of approximately $8 per year! It is a little difficult to express such an in-
flow as a ratio of GDP or investment since the former is in
foreign exchange while the latter is in overvalued rupees.
Without making such an adjustment, capital inflow would be
around 1·2 per cent of GDP and perhaps about 10 per cent of
gross investment. For Pakistan the corresponding figures would
be about 6 per cent of GDP and half of gross investment! Thus,
even during the period of her peak rate of capital inflow, the
Bangladesh economy was highly self-reliant by the standard
not only of Pakistan, which was excessively dependent on
external aid, but also by the standards of most other developing
economies.

  Imports were largely devoted to the purchase of capital goods
and materials for capital goods (steel and cement). Much of the
fuel also had to be imported. Finally there was the burden of a
food deficit which in a bad year could claim nearly 20 per cent
of available foreign exchange.

  [1] One way to consider the situation is to think that of the aid received
from the donor nations, the amount over and above Rs. 78 million was *tied*
to the Pakistan market, as a result of which the real value of aid to Bangladesh was less to the extent that goods were overpriced in that market.

9 Private and Public Saving

9.1 SOME INTRODUCTORY COMMENTS

WHEN it comes to the question of generating an investible surplus, all conventional development theorists would probably tend to despair of the prospects for Bangladesh. The modern capitalist sector, which plays such an important role in many models of capital accumulation, is a tiny proportion of the economy. Its share would be below 15 per cent of GDP even when allowances are made for modern transport and trade besides large- and medium-scale industries, banking, insurance and power. Even if this sector saves at a high rate (a big *if* in view of the performance in the past in Bangladesh and Pakistan during their political association) such savings would not amount to a very large proportion of GDP.

The remaining sectors largely take the form of subsistence economic activities. This applies to agriculture, the cottage industries and the subsistence services. Conventional development theory does not picture these sectors as areas of dynamic accumulation. Peasant agriculture does not have the Middle Eastern or Latin American kind of concentration of consumption which could be channelled into accumulation by a few bold reforms.

There are many models of growth which emphasise the inevitability of subjecting agriculture to a period of 'primitive capital accumulation' in spite of the sector's relative (and certainly absolute) poverty. The argument usually is that unless a reasonably high rate of saving can be imposed on this vast sector, no respectable overall saving rate can be achieved for the economy as a whole. Even if one were a believer in this kind of strategy, one would need to pause in the context of Bangladesh. This is because the poor agricultural sector of this poorest of the poor nations has in recent times been already subjected once to ruthless 'primitive capital accumulation' for the industrialisation of West Pakistan. Such accumulation has been made both by imposing (*a*) a high concealed tax (apart from moderate open taxation) on the sector by making it surrender its very high foreign exchange earnings at an artificially-kept low price in terms of domestic rupees, (*b*) by making the sector buy goods in the protected domestic market at an artificially inflated price and (*c*) by imposing a net surplus in the sector's transactions with the rest of the economy through absentee ownership, unfavourable balance between Government revenue and expenditure in rural areas, and other means. Aspects (*a*) and (*b*) have been discussed above in various chapters. Preliminary estimates show that aspect (*c*) was also very important quantitatively.[1] One would naturally wonder about the implications both for equity and efficiency of subjecting the sector so soon to another phase of ruthless accumulation.

9.2 RATES OF PERSONAL SAVING

The resources that were generated in agriculture by the above means were saved involuntarily and transferred to finance various activities in non-agricultural sectors (mostly in West Pakistan). But what was the extent of voluntary saving either in the form of direct capital construction or in the conversion of current income into monetary or real assets of some kind?

Asbjorn Bergan's estimates were a bit of a sensation when they appeared in 1967.[2] On the basis of the information provided in the national sample survey for 1963/64[3] and after a careful scrutiny for the consistency of the definitions of income, consumption and saving, Bergan arrived at the following estimates of personal saving rates (before income tax) in Bangladesh (then East Pakistan):

> Rural households   12 per cent of income
> Urban households   9·9 per cent of income

These are very high rates, particularly for rural households. If these rates could obtain over a long period and be matched

[1] See Keith Griffin, 'Financing Development Plans in Pakistan', *The Pakistan Development Review*, winter 1965. Griffin analyses this aspect for the whole of the then Pakistan, of which Bangladesh was a part.

[2] See Asbjorn Bergan, 'Personal Income Distribution and Personal savings in Pakistan: 1963/64', *The Pakistan Development Review*, summer 1967.

[3] These surveys, carried out by the CSO, are called the *Quarterly Survey of Current Economic Conditions*.

by a suitable rate of saving in the corporate sector, the economy of Bangladesh could take off along the path of self-sustained growth. While some saw in these estimates the demolition of the argument that poor peasants cannot save, others were sceptical about the statistical basis of the measurement. Particularly puzzling was the fact that the considerably poorer rural households were significantly higher savers than the urban households.

To resolve the puzzle one needed more observations and estimates of saving rates. This is what we set ourselves to do on the basis of the information in the *Quarterly Survey of Current Economic Conditions* (QSCEC) for the year 1966/67.[1] The 1966/67 QSCEC had made substantial improvements in defining income, consumption and saving (perhaps largely learning from Bergan's criticism) and we made some further adjustments to conform to Bergan's concepts.[2] The rates of personal saving that we estimated for 1966/67 are as follows:

> Rural households $-1·12$ per cent of income
> Urban households $4·03$ per cent of income

These rates have not even a remote resemblance to the 1963/64 rates estimated by Bergan. Either one has to conclude that the saving rates estimated from the QSCEC are subject to such extraordinarily large errors that they are useless, or one must find some plausible explanation of their extreme variability. In trying to do the latter, we put together the following information about the two years for which we have the savings estimates:

	Percentage change in 1963/64 over the year before	*Percentage change in 1966/67 over the year before*
1. Production of rice	$+19·8$	$-8·8$
2. Value added in agriculture	$+9·5$	$-2·7$
3. Value added in major crops	$+15·0$	$-6·3$
4. GDP per capita	$+7·3$	$-1·7$

[1] The survey remained unpublished until the time the author lost contact with Pakistan's CSO (in mid-1971), but the manuscript tables had been made available to him through the courtesy of the Director-General of the CSO.

[2] Perhaps there still remained some very minor discrepancy, e.g. we could not identify 'other sources' of income. But they were only $0·8$ per cent of total.

The above information suggests some explanation. In 1963/64 there was a very big jump in agricultural production after a disastrous and flood-devastated year. It was natural that farmers would take advantage of the unusual circumstances to build up the assets lost in the disaster of the previous year and accumulate some additional assets as well.[1] Thus the saving rate would naturally be higher than it would be on the average in a year of average income.

The year 1966/67 was the exact opposite. There was a sharp decline in agricultural output and income. The farmers would naturally be unable to finance their aggregate consumption and investment needs by their current income. They would have to sell assets, withdraw past savings and borrow. Indeed, the QSCEC of 1966/67 shows that on the average rural households obtained an additional 7·7 per cent of their income to finance the excess of their current consumption and investment needs over current income from the following sources:

> Sale of property   = 2·73 per cent of income
> Withdrawal of savings = 1·34 per cent of income
> Borrowing and others = 3·62 per cent of income

We did not have access to the unpublished background material of the 1963/64 QSCEC to check whether there was a build-up of real and financial assets and liquidation of debt, but we expect that they did happen.

What picture does emerge from the savings estimates for two very unusual (but dissimilar) years? We can be reasonably confident that under normal circumstances farmers would not save as much as in the unusually good year of 1963/64 when they had a lot to build up because of the devastation of the previous year. We can be equally certain that, except for a sharp and sudden decline in income and output as in 1966/67, the farmers would be unlikely to save at a negative rate. What the average saving rate in years with normal incomes would be cannot be ascertained with any confidence without some more observed estimates. But in view of the fact that the average year is probably characterised by something like the average of the circumstances of the two years under review (i.e. with

---

[1] Bergan himself refers to the possibility of such an explanation.

modest positive rates of increase in income and output), it is tempting to argue that the rate of saving on the average would be somewhat around the average of the rates for 1963/64 and 1966/67, i.e. between 4 and 6 per cent.

Another tentative hypothesis that might be drawn is the possibility of a high incremental saving rate. The fact that the high incomes following a particularly bad year were not largely consumed shows that the peasants are aware of the need to replace capital assets, and that; if provided with attractive investment opportunities of sufficiently divisible size, they will probably respond by saving at quite reasonable rates.

The decline in the urban saving rate in 1966/67 over what was observed in 1963/64 is much milder and hence quite easy to explain with reference to the same facts. Although the non-agricultural sectors did not do particularly badly, the rise in the prices of rice and food meant a decline in real income. Also, the interaction between urban and rural households is significant. In a good crop year an urban wage- (or salary-) earning household receives a net income transfer from the bit of land it may hold in absentee ownership. In a bad crop year such receipts decline and perhaps more families have to remit more income to feed the relations left behind.

9.3 PUBLIC SAVING

Until Bangladesh emerged as an independent nation, the provincial government, then the Government of East Pakistan (GOEP), had few financial powers. Customs, sales, excise, income and corporation taxes were all exclusively raised by the Central Pakistan Government. The GOEP used to get a share of the revenue from these taxes. Land revenue was about the only important tax raised by the provincial Government. It does not appear particularly useful to analyse the revenue and expenditure position of the GOEP in the past. To get some idea of the likely budgetary situation to be faced by the Bangladesh Government in the near future, it is much more meaningful to estimate the revenues that an independent government could raise and the expenditures that such a government would have to incur. To avoid making a host of projections of the levels of various economic activities, we carry out the exercise for a past year, the most recent one for which we have all the relevant information, 1968/69.

A possible state of affairs of the budgetary position of an independent government of Bangladesh in 1968/69 is shown in Table 9.1. The exercise is a highly speculative and unreal one; it pictures an imaginary situation in which production, import and export take place roughly as they did in 1968/69 while an independent government collects taxes roughly at the existing rates (with some adjustments) and spends for the maintenance of roughly the kind of activities it is likely to perform now. Such an exercise, though imaginary, is instructive in shedding light on the likely budgetary situation of the Bangladesh Government in future.

Customs revenue in the former Pakistan in 1968/69 had reached 34 per cent of the value of c.i.f. imports. Had Bangladesh been independent in 1968/69, regional imports also would have provided customs duty though their c.i.f. value would perhaps be no more than two-thirds of what it was. Customs revenue has been estimated by us at 33 per cent of the estimated total of c.i.f. imports.

TABLE 9·1

A POSSIBLE STATE OF THE BUDGETARY POSITION
POSITION OF AN INDEPENDENT GOVERNMENT
OF BANGLADESH IN 1968/69
(*million rupees*)

Revenue

Existing revenue of GOEP	856
Customs duty	888
Sales and excise taxes	951
Income and corporation tax	111
Income from post, telegraph, civil administration etc.	196
Estimated earning from public sector enterprises	348
	3,350

Expenditure

Existing expenditure of GOEP	1,680
(Less debt service to Central Government)	– 478
Additional Public Administration and Government	600
Defence	300
	2,102
Revenue surplus	1,248
(approximately 4·6% of GDP)	

Sales and excise taxes of the former Pakistan had been 10·5 per cent of the value of the base, which we define as the sum of the gross value of output of organised industries and the value of all imports. We have applied the same rate to the estimated base in Bangladesh. Income and corporation tax were just over 1 per cent of the non-agricultural part of GDP; we have taken 1 per cent of the same in Bangladesh.

As a consequence of the independence of Bangladesh, a very high proportion of the industrial and financial enterprises formerly owned by (West) Pakistanis would become public sector enterprises. Including the existing Industrial Development Corporation-owned enterprises, these will give the Government ownership of over two-thirds of the 2(j) factories, banks etc. The post-tax profits from these enterprises at the 1968/69 rate has been estimated to be Rs. 348 million.

On the expenditure side a wild guess has been made about the cost of additional administration including foreign affairs – at 600 million it is more than one and a half times the 395 million the provincial Government spent on general administration, police, education and health. On defence, the Bangladesh Government cannot sensibly spend more than say, Rs. 300 million. Bangladesh has a common border almost entirely with friendly India, except for about 100 miles of mountainous border with nearly equally friendly Burma. The Government leaders have already expressed the intention of spending on defence a very small proportion of total revenue.

The other important factor in expenditure is the cessation of the payment of the huge debt service to the central government which had crippled the budgetary position of the provincial government in the past. Rather than distributing the sources of revenue between the centre and the provinces in a way to allow each to balance its budget, a deliberate imbalance was created by keeping with the centre more revenue than it needed to balance its budget. Over the years the centre 'lent' to the province and thus created a huge debt service burden amounting to more than half the GOEP revenue by 1968/69. The whole exercise seems to have been a strange book-keeping charade because – and this could not happen in a true federation – the provincial governments since 1958 had been the direct appointees of and solely responsible to the central government.

With the independence of Bangladesh this drain is finally stopped.

Thus the Bangladesh government ends up with a high rate of surplus to be invested for the growth of the economy; public saving, at 4·6 per cent of the GDP, would allow the government to launch a significant development effort. There is, of course, no mystery behind this favourable prognosis. An independent Bangladesh can afford to avoid one of the biggest wastes that the subcontinental neighbours suffered from, wasteful defence spending. She can also do away with the burden of debt service to the central government. With such significant economies, even the modest means of taxation existing in the former Pakistan would enable the government to generate quite a large surplus.

If, however, Bangladesh settles for a *per capita* military expenditure of the proportion obtaining in India or the former Pakistan, the entire surplus would be wiped out. In view of the crucial importance of the issue, it may be worth while to cross for a moment the traditional borders of an economist's domain. It is difficult to specify the factors that regulate the volume of military expenditure since so many subjective and external factors dominate. However, if one were to specify the objective factors that a rational society ought to be guided by, priority will probably be assigned to the length of the actually or potentially hostile border. Given this and the physical military programme implied by it, the actual budget will depend on factors like the wage rate.

Bangladesh has a common border with only two countries, Burma (about a 100 miles of difficult terrain) and India. The

TABLE 9·2

MILITARY EXPENDITURE IN SELECTED COUNTRIES

	Million Dollars at Official Exchange Rates
Ceylon (1968)	12·7
Afghanistan (1968)	27·3
Nepal (1968)	6·6
Burma (1969)	110·7

SOURCE
Stockholm International Peace Research Institute, *SIPRI Yearbook of World Armaments and Disarmament 1969/70* (Stockholm, 1970).

relationship with both countries is extremely friendly. It may be argued that it is not impossible that at some future date the friendliness with India may become strained. But it would be futile to think in terms of safeguarding the independence of Bangladesh militarily against India if ever the need arose. The best deterrent for such a possibility is certainly the popular basis of the Bangladesh government and sensible international diplomacy.

The countries listed in Table 9.2 are all located with significantly more sensitive borders than Bangladesh. And yet with the exception of Burma their military budgets have been way below what is being provided for Bangladesh in Table 9.1. Even in per capita terms, all the countries in the table except Burma (which had special difficulties) spent less than what we have specified for Bangladesh.

There will certainly be formidable pressures against such a sensible defence policy. Internally, many will be haunted by the spectre of subversion. Again, such 'subversion' can become a danger only when the Government have lost the confidence of the vast majority who have been won over by the 'insurgents'. If ever the Bangladesh government adopts such a policy of suppressing 'internal subversion' by military means by recruiting a vast army, there will be nothing to hope for its economic future.

There is also the probable pressure from outside. Bangladesh is situated in a sensitive part of the world. Superpowers have been engaged in endless games of setting up alliances against each other in this area. There will no doubt be pressures to become part of one or the other 'defensive wall,' either openly or secretly. If Bangladesh succumbs to such pressure, the hope of limiting defence expenditure will be ended once for all. Although the circumstances of the emergence of Bangladesh are not particularly helpful in withstanding such pressure, can one hope that the clear declaration of Prime Minister Sheikh Mujib in his very first press conference in January 1972 that 'Bangladesh will be the Switzerland of the East' is an indication of both the understanding of and the arrival at a correct solution to the crucial problem?

What about the debt service to the former central government in the unlikely event of a negotiated settlement between Bangladesh and Pakistan about the distribution of assets and liabilities? The West Pakistan government had a similar debt to the central government, its debt service burden in 1968/69 being Rs. 431 million, only a little less than the amount paid by Bangladesh. To the extent that Bangladesh has a claim to the former central government assets, the solution would be to cancel that against her indebtedness, thus wiping out what after all is a book-keeping contrivance.

What about the burden of external debt? Even if one goes by the nominal location of aid-financed projects and the direction of aid-backed imports, the share of Bangladesh would be low, somewhere around 25 per cent of the massive debt of former Pakistan (standing at $3149 million in July 1970). But the known position of the Bangladesh economists and politicians has been that to obtain the real magnitude of the aid-flow one has to subtract from the nominal aid inflow the loss due to its 'tying' to West Pakistan and perhaps also the resource transfer caused by the former Pakistan government. If Bangladesh and Pakistan ever come to face each other across a conference table to resolve this issue, there is going to be some hard bargaining involving all physical assets of the former central government. Since there is no clear precedent in modern history, it is difficult to see the outline of the final outcome.

Part III

Planning for the Future

10 An Overall View of Sectoral Priorities

10.1 PRODUCTION PLANNING AND SCARCITY PRICES

PERHAPS one could describe the problem of development planning as that of finding answers to two interrelated questions: the first is to define the best possible combination of the output capacities of various production activities and the second is to estimate the 'scarcity prices' which must be obeyed if the best possible allocation of resources is to be achieved. It is not really enough to be able to define the production plan since its implementation, even in a fully planned economy, will require decision-making at a large number of different levels at which central directive alone, unaccompanied by a suitable system of indicators of scarcities, is not likely to prove adequate. In the kind of 'mixed economy' that Bangladesh appears to have opted for, a large number of private decision-making units will co-exist with public sector planning. In this context, the proper use of resources and the implementation of the production plan will be crucially dependent on the identification of and obedience to scarcity prices.

It has been customary to solve these problems by the application of linear programming techniques. The production plan is derived by maximising some objective function (e.g. national income, aggregate consumption) subject to the supply and demand balance constraints for individual activities and overall resources. The dual of the linear programming solution provides a set of shadow prices. By now a large number of such models are available for the developing economies.

A major problem of this approach is that the linearity of the models, due both to the limitation on the availability of the methods of solution and of the statistical information necessary to estimate non-linear relations, leads to extreme solutions indicating concentration of production in only a few sectors.

Since such extreme solutions are obviously unfeasible for practical considerations, the models in actual practice have tended to introduce *ad hoc* constraints, usually on the levels of exports, the requirements of imports and the maximum feasible rates of output expansion ('absorption capacities') in particular activities, to prevent such extreme outcomes.

Such practices predetermine much of a country's comparative advantage and severely limits the role of optimising procedures in deciding whether a particular good ought to be produced, produced and exported, or imported. Thus, although such models profess to determine the optimum pattern of comparative advantage, in practice much of it is specified exogenously and arbitrarily. The shadow prices in the dual merely become an even more remote reflection of some arbitrary constraint postulated in the primal model.

In this chapter our purpose is to present some general notions of the sectoral priority in production planning by having some idea in outline about which products are socially most profitable as exports; which are just profitable enough to deserve production for domestic use; and which are so expensive to produce as to be better imported. We do not adopt the usual programming approach, because of the problems outlined above. Instead we apply a model developed jointly by Professor J. A. Mirrlees and the present author, which solves the problem in an alternative way.[1]

The emphasis of the model is on allowing the forces of social comparative advantage to have full play. We have therefore devised a method of measuring the social cost of production, marginal import cost and marginal export revenue of each product in a common unit of valuation so that from the comparison of the three a decision can be taken whether it is socially desirable to produce the commodity, produce and export, or import.

---

[1] A full treatment of the model and its application is awaiting publication at some date in the near future. While there is no intention on the part of the writer to attribute responsibility for the present exposition to Professor Mirrlees, he would like to state that the idea of the model was originally conceived by him.

10.2 A STATEMENT OF THE MODEL

The starting point of the model is the valuation of the social cost of production which, compared to the corresponding import cost and export revenue, serves as the basis of deciding whether the commodity ought to be produced or not and of quantifying the accounting price. To emphasise the price-cost aspect of the model, the comparison of which serves to define the production pattern, we call it a 'Model of Accounting Prices' (MAP).

10.2.1 *The components of cost*

We begin by enumerating the elements of cost of production from the standpoint of the society. We broadly classify the costs into those inputs purchased in the domestic market and those purchased from abroad and paid for in terms of foreign exchange. Since domestic prices are not representative of true social scarcities,[1] we would want to re-evaluate all purchases in the domestic market at some common set of denominators in terms of 'foreign exchange equivalents', called accounting prices.

First, we have the foreign exchange equivalent of current inputs purchased domestically. The trade, transport and other service inputs used up in taking the imported inputs from the port of entry to the using sector are included in the domestic purchase of current inputs. Repair and maintenance of capital inputs are also accounted for.

The next element of cost is the interest on physical capital purchased from domestic producers. This includes all buildings, fixed capital goods purchased domestically and inventory of domestically-produced raw materials and products – all evaluated at accounting prices.

---

[1] This is a well-known phenomenon and has been referred to in Chapter 6. As a result of direct trade and economic controls arbitrarily imposed, the price structure loses all correspondence to social scarcities and indeed scarcities in world trade. Literature on effective protection is full of discussion of the phenomenon. See Ian Little, Tibor Scitovsky and Maurice Scott, *Industry and Trade* (Oxford University Press, 1970), for general reference.

A good deal of controversy surrounds the question of labour cost in a developing economy of the type of Bangladesh. The range that is usually considered is between the marginal product of labour in traditional employment and the consumption of workers in new employment. In Bangladesh the latter would be considerably in excess of the former. The labour cost can be as low as the former only under the assumption that commitment to additional consumption is no cost to the society. This is hardly plausible in view of the shortage of savings in an economy like Bangladesh. The labour cost can be as high as the workers' consumption only under the extreme assumption that there is no virtue in increasing consumption *now* and that all that matters now is to generate surplus to increase consumption at some future date. Again, there is little justification for such an extreme position particularly in view of the widespread poverty today. Where exactly between the two limits the social cost of labour should lie would obviously depend on such factors as the society's preference between present and future consumption, the expected length of the period during which the society will have the problem of inadequate savings and the rate of return on new investment. Little and Mirrlees found that on plausible assumptions with respect to each of these, shadow wage is a fairly high proportion of the value of workers' consumption. They also found that the proportion is relatively insensitive to quite large variations in the quantitative assumptions with respect to the factors listed above. This is a reassuring feature of their method and also rather convincing.[1]

It may be useful to emphasise that there are two steps in estimating the social cost of labour. First, the workers' consumption of domestic goods would have to be re-evaluated at accounting prices. The next step is to apply the shadow wage *ratio* to the value of workers' consumption at accounting prices to obtain the shadow wage *rate*.

Our next element of cost is consumption by capitalists, which is treated as the cost of private enterprise; unlike that for workers, no part of capitalists' consumption is exempted from being treated as social cost as there would be little virtue in increasing the consumption of those who already have a high

[1] Ian Little and James Mirrlees, *Manual of Industrial Project Analysis in Developing Countries*, vol. II (OECD, 1969).

standard of living relative to the average for the society. Again, the consumptive goods supplied by the domestic producers will have to be re-evaluated at accounting prices.

We next have to consider the elements of cost directly incurred in foreign exchange; the c.i.f. value of all current inputs, the accounting rate of interest times the c.i.f. value of all fixed and working capital inputs, the shadow wage ratio times the value of the few imported goods consumed by the workers, and finally the (not so few) imported goods consumed by the capitalists, all at c.i.f. values. We have included imports from (then West) Pakistan in these 'direct foreign exchange' outlays after converting them at appropriate c.i.f. prices.

In the usual multisectoral models, the cost of land for agricultural activities is not included in the specification of inputs. This leads to an artificially high estimate of the rate of return (calculated as the ratio of profit to the value of capital inputs) in agriculture since a good deal of such 'profit' should be treated as rent to land. After a careful evaluation of the possible alternative methods, we decided to assume that land supply can be augmented and that some production function can be postulated for such activity. It is easy to anticipate objections to this approach: how plausible is the assumption of such a fixed production function? Would not the cost be an increasing function of the supply of cropped acreage? Are not the irrigation and reclamation projects typically large and indivisible?

However appealing the objections may appear, a close scrutiny proves them no more formidable than the objections to the standard linear models of applied planning. We have already suggested that a quite significant increase in cropped acreage can be obtained by the use of surface and ground water which ensures a fairly steady cost per acre. It is of course undeniable that this cannot be done without limit, but there should be no overwhelming problem for quite a significant range (see Chapter 5).

Our method essentially is to estimate all current capital and labour inputs by the use of which cropped acreage can be increased by the amount required per unit of output of any agricultural sector. Such inputs are then added to the direct inputs into the sector.

112 *Planning for the Future*

p_j = accounting price index (i.e. the ratio of accounting price to market price) for the product of sector j;

a_{ij} = value of current input produced domestically by sector i used per unit of output of sector j;

b_{ij} = fixed and working capital supplied by domestic production in sector i for unit expansion in output capacity in sector j;

c_{ij} = purchase of domestic i sector's goods for consumption per unit of wage in sector j;

g_{ij} = purchase of domestic i sector's goods for consumption per unit of profit earned in sector j;

a_j = c.i.f. value of all imported current inputs used by sector j;

b_j = c.i.f. value of all imported capital inputs used by sector j;

c_j = c.i.f. value of all imported consumption goods purchased per unit of wage in j;

g_j = c.i.f. value of all imported consumption goods purchased per unit of profit earned in j;

w_j = wage cost per unit of output in sector j;

z_j = profit per unit of output in sector j;

λ = shadow wage as a proportion of workers' consumption evaluated at accounting prices;

r = accounting rate of interest;

p_j^m = marginal import cost index of the product of sector j; and

p_j^e = marginal export revenue index of the product of sector j.

10.2.2. *The model of accounting prices*

Now we are able to state formally the components of the accounting cost of production (denoted by π_j for sector j) by using the notation of Table 10.1. Note that the π_j is not the unit cost of production but the index of accounting cost, i.e. the accounting cost of producing that quantity of output j which sells for a unit of value at market price. The same meaning would apply to p_j the accounting price index. Our equation for accounting cost of production for sector j is:

$$\pi_j = \sum_i a_{ij}\, p_i + r\sum_i b_{ij}\, p_i + \lambda w_j \sum_i c_{ij}\, p_i$$
$$+ z_j \sum_i g_{ij}\, p_i + a_j + rb_j + \lambda w_j c_j + z_j g_j$$

Under complete autarky, accounting prices would be the same as accounting costs. But if there are trading possibilities it would be cheaper to import a good which has a marginal import cost smaller than the accounting cost of production. In such a case, the accounting price would obviously be the import cost. If the import cost is higher than the accounting cost of production, it would pay to produce the commodity domestically and the accounting price would be the same as the accounting cost.

However little the accounting cost be, a good will always be worth at least what it can be sold for in the international market. Thus the marginal export revenue would provide the floor; if the accounting cost is less than or equal to export revenue, it would pay to export the good and the accounting price would be the same as export revenue.

The relevant export revenue would be the f.o.b. price of export, replaced by marginal revenue in the case of the goods in which the Bangladesh share in world exports is large (jute, jute textiles and tea). The c.i.f. cost is the import cost at the port of entry. To this must be added the cost of domestic trade and transport inputs required to take the commodity to its users. These inputs would of course have to be evaluated at their accounting prices.

We can now provide a complete statement of the equation system of the model:

(1) $p_j = \min \{\pi_j, (p_j^m + p_s m_j + p_s' m_j')\}$

subject to:

(2) $p_j \geq p_j^s$ and

(3) $p_j = p_j^e$ for any n sectors;

Sector j ought to produce domestically if:

$$\pi_j \leq (p_j^m + p_s m_j + p_s' m_j'),$$

be imported if:

$$\pi_j > (p_j^m + p_s m_j + p_s' m_j'),$$

and exported if:

$$\pi_j \leq p_j^e,$$

where $p_s (p_s') = $ accounting price of the service produced by domestic transport (trade) sector,

and $m_j (m_j') = $ transport (trade) service required per unit of import of the j th type.

In other words, the accounting price is either the accounting cost or the import cost, whichever is lower, subject to the condition that they are at least as high as the export revenue and exactly as high as the export revenue for n sectors. This last condition determines the ARI (the accounting rate of interest).

To explain, let us for the moment define the constraint (3) as requiring that only one good be exported. The method of solution is as follows: a trial value of ARI is selected for which the main equations (1) are solved by iteration to give the accounting prices. These accounting prices are compared with the export prices. If all accounting prices are greater than the corresponding export prices, a smaller ARI is chosen; if some accounting price is lower than the corresponding export price, a higher ARI is chosen. Since the accounting prices are positively monotonic functions of the ARI, this kind of change is in the right direction to approach final solution. The trials continue until the point is reached at which the condition is exactly satisfied. To obtain a solution with two (or more) exports, the system is solved by putting the export revenue (p_j^e) equal to zero for the original export(s), i.e. pretending that the best export is not exportable (since we are sure it is) to force the model to throw up the next best export.

10.2.3 *Sector classification and data*

To apply the model to Bangladesh, we divided the economy into 29 sectors shown in Table 10.2. This sector classification is perhaps too highly aggregated for many detailed investigations. Many of the sectors, particularly the ones of the residual type, would be too heterogeneous to make the results applicable to any but the commodities in the sector which conform to the average conditions of the sector. Our difficulty was due to the limited detail in which intersectoral data are available for the Bangladesh economy. While the present classification is not the best for detailed planning of the production structure, it is adequate to give an overall idea of the priorities and can serve a useful purpose for many detailed analyses if the results are carefully applied in combination with supplementary information.

TABLE 10.2

SECTOR CLASSIFICATION

1. Rice	16. Chemicals
2. Jute	17. Cement
3. Tea	18. Basic metal
4. All other agriculture (AOA)	19. Metal products
5. Sugar	20. Machinery
6. Edible oils	21. Transport equipment
7. Cigarettes	22. Miscellaneous manufacturing
8. Miscellaneous food	23. Construction
9. Cotton textiles	24. Electricity and gas
10. Jute textiles	25. Transport
11. Miscellaneous textiles	26. Trade
12. Paper	27. Housing
13. Leather and leather products	28. Government
14. Rubber products	29. Miscellaneous service
15. Fertiliser	

The intersectoral data have been based on the studies carried out at the Bangladesh (then Pakistan) Institute of Development Economics[1] with suitable further adjustments to fit the requirements of the present model. Although the basic data refer to 1962/63, adjustments were made to reflect the incremental structure in the mid-sixties by incorporating information from the later CMIs. The input structures of the manufacturing industries (sectors 5 to 22) mostly refer to modern large- and medium-scale industries with some (modern) small-scale industries included in cotton textiles and the residual sectors.

Workers' consumption pattern has been estimated from that of the appropriate urban expenditure groups in the Quarterly Surveys of Current Economic Conditions and the capitalists' consumption pattern from that of the highest expenditure group in urban areas in the Survey. The import costs and export revenues have been estimated from the detailed studies available

[1] The important ones are by A. R. Khan and A. MacEwan, *Regional Current Input-Output Tables for East and West Pakistan Economies, 1962/63,* J. J. Stern, *Inter-industry Relations in East Pakistan 1962/63,* A. R. Khan and A. MacEwan, 'A Multisectoral Analysis of Capital Requirement for Development Planning in Pakistan', the *Pakistan Development Review,* winter 1967, and A. R. Khan, *Some Methodological Problems of the Treatment of Imports and Consumption in Multisectoral Models of Planning and Growth.*

on these measurements.[1] For raw jute, jute textiles and tea marginal export revenues have been adjusted downward on the basis of estimated elasticities in view of the high average share of Bangladesh in world exports.

10.2.4 *Some results of the model*

For a given shadow wage ratio and a given number of exports (decided by balance of payments considerations) the model tells us (*a*) the pattern of domestic production, import and export (note that the series of exports are endogenously provided by the model, all that has to be done from outside is to decide the cut-off point); (*b*) the accounting prices for the products of various sectors; and (*c*) the ARI, the social rate of return. For a given solution, we can estimate for each sector, the social rate of return as follows:

$$\frac{p_j - \sum_i a_{ij} p_i - \lambda w_j \sum_i c_{ij} p_i - z_j \sum_i g_{ij} p_i - a_j - \lambda w_j c_j - z_j g_j}{\sum_i b_{ij} p_i + b_j}$$

where the numerator shows the value of social profit per unit of output and the denominator shows the value of all capital at accounting prices per unit of output. Note that for all sectors which are domestically produced (and exported), the social rate of return is the same as ARI (excepting insignificant differences due to the less than perfect accuracy demanded in computations to save time). This is because for such sectors $p_j = \pi_j$ (see equation 1 above) and the equation for π_j requires the sectoral rates of return to be equal (and equal, in turn, to ARI). For the sectors which ought to have been imported, but are being produced because of the wrong incentive system, the social rate of return will be less than ARI since for them $p_j =$ marginal import cost $< \pi_j$.

In tables 10.3 and 10.4 we obtain alternative solutions of the

---

[1] Pal, M. L., 'The Determinants of the Domestic Prices of Imports', in the *Pakistan Development Review* (PDR), winter 1964; Alamgir, M., 'The Domestic Prices of Imported Commodities in Pakistan', *PDR*, spring 1968; Islam, N., 'Commodity Exports, Net Exchange Earnings and Investment Criteria', *PDR*, winter 1968, and Soligo, R. and J. J. Stern, 'Some Comments on the Export Bonus, Export Promotion and Investment Criteria', *PDR*, spring 1966.

model by varying the shadow wage ratio and the number of exports. After an analysis of the alternative solutions we pick up a basic solution for which the details of comparative advantage, accounting prices, and social rates of return are shown in Table 10.5.

Table 10.3 shows the effect of the variation in shadow wage ratio from 1 to zero in discrete steps. We should like to draw attention to the effect of such variation on the ARI, the production structure and the sectoral accounting prices. The ARI is rather sensitive to variation in the shadow wage ratio since workers' consumption is an important element of cost although much less so than in a developed economy with high wage-rates.

A decline in the shadow wage ratio changes the sectoral accounting prices through the interplay of two opposing effects. It reduces the labour cost which tends to pull down the accounting cost of production. But a lower shadow wage ratio means a higher ARI which, through higher interest cost on capital, tends to push up the accounting price. The balance of the two effects would depend on the structure of production in a given sector, i.e. the greater the importance of labour (capital) cost, the stronger will be the downward pull (upward push) through the reduction in labour cost (the increased interest cost). Thus the labour-intensive sectors will emerge relatively better-off as a result of a decline in the shadow wage ratio. In reality, the push of increased interest is almost invariably stronger than the pull of the decreased labour cost; a decline in the shadow wage ratio raises the sectoral accounting prices (residual agricultural sector being the only exception).

As the accounting costs rise across the board, the effect on the production plan is clear: at lower shadow wage ratios fewer sectors are profitable enough for domestic production. This is particularly true for the relatively capital-costly manufacturing sectors. While 11 (10) of the 22 tradeable sectors are profitable enough to be produced domestically at the shadow wage ratio of 1 (0·875), only 5 (3) remain so at the shadow wage ratio of 0·5 (zero). Even more remarkable is the fact that only two manufacturing sectors remain profitable at a shadow wage ratio of 0·5 and none at zero.

We have opted for a fairly high shadow wage ratio of $\frac{7}{8}$ (0·875) for our basic solution. The reason basically is that in spite of the low current consumption, the acute shortage of capital and its high productivity in an economy like that of Bangladesh would dictate relatively high weight to current saving.[1]

Also we find that much lower ratios would imply production structures which would be unfeasible from many practical considerations. Such production structures would imply extreme specialisation in favour of agriculture, thereby defeating the objective of expanding non-agricultural employment which is often the reason that leads people to argue for a low shadow wage.

Note, however, that the shadow wage *rate* would be lower since the value of workers' consumption at the accounting price would be lower than the market wage partly because workers may save a little but more importantly because the accounting value of the consumption bundle $(\Sigma c_{ij} p_i + c_j)$ would be less than at the market price $(\Sigma c_{ij} + c_j)$. For workers in jute textiles, the accounting value of consumption is just under 55 per cent of the market wage, so that the shadow wage would be a mere 48 per cent of the market wage.

Capitalists' consumption is not included as a cost in the usual kind of benefit-cost analysis although there are some methods which in principle argue for its inclusion.[2] There, however, seems little argument for exempting it when much of the workers' consumption is treated as cost. As is shown in Table 10.3 (last column) the effect of excluding capitalists' consumption from cost is somewhat similar to that of lowering the shadow wage ratio with one important exception: the manufacturing sectors are relatively at a smaller disadvantage than when the shadow wage ratio is reduced.

The idea that all the foreign exchange need can be met from a single export is unrealistic since the assumption of fixed marginal export revenue is plausible for only a limited increase in exports. It would, therefore, be natural to look for additional export sectors. As already mentioned, this is done in the present method of solution by putting the export price(s) of the original

---

[1] See Little and Mirrlees, op. cit., for very illuminating discussions on why the value of the shadow wage ratio ought to be high and how this high proportion remains little affected by wide variations in underlying conditions. In fact 0·875 is the lower of the values they consider plausible.

[2] See Little and Mirrlees, op. cit., pp. 94–5.

export sector(s) equal to zero and obtaining a further solution of the model. In fact, in the drive for an additional export good, the process tends to improve the trade gap in several ways. First, some new sector becomes profitable enough for export. Secondly, the accounting price(s) of the previously identified export(s) go below the previous export price(s) so that larger quantities of such exports could be sold abroad.

But additional exports can only be achieved through a reduction in accounting prices in general which in turn means that more sectors become profitable enough for domestic production. This process of import substitution helps further to close the trade gap.

Table 10.4 shows the successive exports. In order of profitability they are: raw jute, tea, leather, jute textiles, cotton textiles and rice. The first four of these are major exports already. The last two are net import commodities today though it is generally recognised that their import substitution will respectively spearhead industrial and agricultural programmes.

What should be the cut-off point? It seems to us that the four exports case is a convenient point because beyond this things seem to be pretty continuous. Several more exports seem to be on the margin of becoming profitable with no change in production plan and little change in ARI and the sectoral accounting prices. Thus foreign exchange supply appears to become pretty elastic at this point. We therefore define this[1] as our basic solution. Table 10.5 shows some detailed features of this 'socially optimal solution'. The fourth column shows the status of each sector from the point of view of comparative advantage: whether the product should be produced and exported, just produced or imported. The last two columns of the table show respectively the market and the social (i.e. all valuations having been made at accounting prices) rates of return for the 29 sectors of the Bangladesh economy.

One of the first observations we can make is that the market rates of return have been extremely bad guides to social profitability. The differences between market and social rates have very high variability. Clearly, the system of incentives

[1] i.e., the case with 0·875 shadow wage ratio, with jute, tea, leather and jute textiles as exports with several others close to being profitable enough to be so and with the capitalists' consumption included in costs.

TABLE 10.3

EFFECT OF VARIATION IN SHADOW WAGE RATIO ON ACCOUNTING PRICES AND PRODUCTION STRUCTURES

(Domestically produced sectors are shown by asterisks, and exports underlined.)

	Capitalists' Consumption Included					Capitalists' Consumption Excluded
SWR	1.000	.875	.750	.500	.000	.875
ARI (Percent)	14.3	19.9	25.6	38.8	78.3	26.3
Accounting Prices						
1. Rice	.748*	.748*	.749*	.750*	.853*	.792*
2. Jute	.696*	.696*	.696*	.695*	.785*	.725*
3. Tea	.617*	.667*	.720*	.840*	.893	.598*
4. AOA	.654*	.628*	.602*	.542*	.443*	.644*
5. Sugar	.391	.397	.403	.413	.454	.389
6. Edible oils	.639*	.663*	.688*	.716	.766	.635*
7. Cigarettes	.320	.324	.329	.336	.365	.319
8. Miscellaneous food	.572*	.591*	.614*	.648	.687	.504*
9. Cotton textiles	.654	.657	.659	.664	.683	.653
10. Jute textiles	.669*	.744*	.825*	.830	.849	.766*
11. Miscellaneous textiles	.512	.515	.519	.525	.551	.510
12. Paper	.576	.579	.583	.589	.613	.575
13. Leather	.598*	.610*	.623*	.644*	.684	.562*
14. Rubber	.566	.573	.581	.595	.650	.562

15. Fertiliser	·947	·958	·970	·995	1·081	·942
16. Chemicals	·462*	·488*	·516*	·574*	·774	·439
17. Cement	·644	·656	·669	·697	·793	·638
18. Basic metals	·644*	·699*	·757*	·847	·932	·694*
19. Metal products	·615	·620	·627	·639	·684	·612
20. Machinery	·645*	·678	·686	·701	·760	·666
21. Transport equipment	·675	·680	·686	·695	·734	·673
22. Misc. manufactures	·525	·530	·536	·547	·589	·522
23. Construction	·579*	·589*	·600*	·610*	·662*	·500*
24. Electricity and Gas	1·717*	2·298*	2·910*	4·313*	9·022*	2·663*
25. Transport	·566*	·664*	·768*	·999*	1·783*	·518*
26. Trade	·726*	·746*	·765*	·792*	·918*	·720*
27. Housing	1·045*	1·349*	1·675*	2·405*	4·900*	1·256*
28. Government	·628*	·668*	·709*	·789*	1·085*	·689*
29. Misc. services	·683*	·715*	·749*	·804*	1·028*	·667*

TABLE 10.4

EFFECT OF INCREASE IN THE NUMBER OF EXPORTS ON ACCOUNTING PRICES AND PRODUCTION STRUCTURE WITH SHADOW WAGE RATIO 0·875

(Domestically produced sectors are shown by asterisks and exports underlined.)

	1 Export 19·9	2 Exports 18·1	3 Exports 16·8	4 Exports 15·9	5 Exports 15·8	6 Exports 15·7
ARI (per cent)						
Accounting Prices:						
1. Rice	·748*	·675*	·616*	·577*	·577*	·567*
2. Jute	·696*	·625*	·568*	·531*	·530*	·520*
3. Tea	·667*	·600*	·545*	·509*	·508*	·499*
4. AOA	·628*	·565*	·513*	·480*	·480*	·471*
5. Sugar	·397	·378	·363	·354	·354	·351
6. Edible oils	·663*	·616*	·578*	·554*	·554*	·547*
7. Cigarettes	·324	·314	·306	·300	·300	·299
8. Misc. food	·591*	·530*	·480*	·449*	·449*	·440*
9. Cotton textiles	·657	·651	·609*	·582*	·581*	·574*
10. Jute textiles	·744*	·664*	·600*	·560*	·559*	·549*
11. Misc. textiles	·515	·502	·492	·486	·486	·484
12. Paper	·579	·572	·566	·562	·562	·561
13. Leather	·610*	·549*	·500*	·468*	·468*	·459*
14. Rubber	·573	·553	·537	·526	·526	·524

15. Fertiliser	·958	·948	·940	·935	·935	·933
16. Chemicals	·486*	·448*	·416*	·395*	·395*	·389*
17. Cement	·656	·643	·632	·626	·626	·624
18. Basic metals	·699*	·650*	·611*	·587*	·586*	·580*
19. Metal products	·620	·608	·598	·577*	·576*	·569*
20. Machinery	·678	·649*	·602*	·572*	·571*	·564*
21. Transport Equipment	·680	·663	·613*	·579*	·578*	·570*
22. Misc. manufactures	·530	·517	·506	·499	·499	·497
23. Construction	·589*	·536*	·492*	·464*	·463*	·456*
24. Electricity and gas	2·298*	2·008*	1·789*	1·649*	1·641*	1·640*
25. Transport	·664*	·589*	·528*	·490*	·488*	·479*
26. Trade	·746*	·661*	·593*	·550*	·549*	·538*
27. Housing	1·349*	1·147*	·996*	·902*	·898*	·876*
28. Government	·668*	·591*	·530*	·491*	·491*	·481*
29. Misc. services	·715*	·633*	·568*	·527*	·526*	·516*

built up by arbitrary and non-uniform protection and numerous policies, direct and indirect, had no correspondence to
social priorities.

The next important observation is that relative to the manufacturing industries, the agricultural sectors appear to have been
discriminated against. The market rates of return for rice and
jute are way below their social rates of return. For tea, the
situation is opposite, but tea is only partly an 'agricultural'
process and even its agricultural part, carried out in plantations,
is vastly different from the usual kind of agricultural organisation. Miscellaneous agriculture is a conglomeration of hetero-
genous activities and is best treated as non-tradeable.

The asymmetrical incentive between agriculture and manufacturing could most convincingly be demonstrated by comparing jute, an agricultural activity, with its own manufacture.
They are both socially profitable enough to be produced and
cheap enough to be exported. But the system of incentives that
prevailed for them in the market as a result of the arbitrary
measures taken by the Government was highly discriminatory.
The market rate of return is less than half the social rate for raw
jute but two-thirds higher than the social rate for jute manufactures. In our discussion of export policies, we have stated at
length the ostensible and real reasons behind such discrimination.

In general, market profit rates have been higher than social
profit rates for the manufacturing industries, though the gap
between the two varies greatly from one sector to another. The
only tradeable sectors for which market profits were lower than
social profit are fertiliser and machinery. This is a bit odd in so
far as both of these are crucial inputs respectively for agricultural and industrial growth. One would expect that market
incentives would be geared to reflect whatever social profitability they might have.

For sugar, cigarettes, miscellaneous textiles and paper, the
social rates of return are negative. The market rates for all of
them are positive and rather high, except for paper.[1]

---

[1] Note that our capital cost is the estimated replacement cost and not the
book values (see Khan, A. R., and A. MacEwan, 'A Multisectoral Analysis
of Capital Requirement for Development Planning', the *Pakistan Development Review*, winter 1967). Accelerated depreciation and other tax benefits

TABLE 10.5

THE BASIC SOLUTION
Shadow Wage Ratio = 0·875
Accounting Rate of Interest = 15·9%

No.	Sector	Accounting Price	Comparative* Advantage	Market Rate Of Return	Social Rate of Return
(1)	(2)	(3)	(4)	(5)	(6)
1.	Rice	0·577	Produce	0·082	0·159
2.	Jute	0·531	Export	0·063	0·159
3.	Tea	0·509	Export	0·251	0·159
4.	Other agriculture	0·480	Produce	0·399	0·158
5.	Sugar	0·354	Import	0·131	−0·074
6.	Edible oil	0·554	Produce	0·391	0·158
7.	Cigarettes	0·300	Import	0·540	−0·385
8.	Other food	0·449	Produce	0·743	0·158
9.	Cotton textile	0·582	Produce	0·198	0·159
10.	Jute textiles	0·560	Export	0·248	0·159
11.	Misc. textiles	0·486	Import	0·124	−0·015
12.	Paper	0·562	Import	0·044	−0·004
13.	Leather	0·468	Export	0·628	0·157
14.	Rubber	0·526	Import	0·218	0·022
15.	Fertiliser	0·935	Import	0·066	0·106
16.	Other Chemicals	0·395	Produce	0·547	0·159
17.	Cement	0·626	Import	0·076	0·068
18.	Basic metals	0·587	Produce	0·257	0·159
19.	Metal products	0·577	Produce	0·202	0·159
20.	Machinery	0·572	Produce	0·150	0·159
21.	Transport equipment	0·579	Produce	0·222	0·159
22.	Misc. manufacturing	0·499	Import	0·164	0·072
23.	Construction	0·464	Non Tradeable	1·908	0·158
24.	Electricity and Gas	1·649	Non Tradeable	0·044	0·159
25.	Transport	0·490	Non Tradeable	0·345	0·159
26.	Trade	0·550	Non Tradeable	0·130	0·159
27.	Housing	0·902	Non Tradeable	0·082	0·159
28.	Government	0·491	Non Tradeable	0·149	0·159
29.	Misc. services	0·527	Non Tradeable	0·205	0·159

* Comparative advantage to 'Produce' means the sector is profitable enough to deserve domestic production to satisfy domestic demand; 'Export' means profitable enough to be produced and exported; and 'Import' means there is no comparative advantage in the production of the good, which should be imported from abroad.

---

may indeed have made the private profit for paper much higher. Since the sector is highly capital-intensive, high depreciation allowances would make a good deal of difference.

For the non-tradeable sectors, the rate of return is the same as ARI. This is because their accounting prices are cost determined (i.e. equal to π) as they cannot be imported however high may the social cost of production be. The cost is defined to cover the accounting interest cost on the social value of capital.

10.3 THE USE OF THE MODEL FOR GUIDANCE IN PLANNING

The exposition of the model should have conveyed the feeling that its authors do not think that all the results should be translated into action unhesitatingly. The degree of aggregation, the tentative character of some data and some of the simplifying assumptions would call for pause before drawing action programmes from the above results. In this section, we shall deal with some of the important problems of application. The first one is about a limitation of the present application of the model (not, hopefully, of the model itself). The model allows full play to the forces of comparative advantage. In order for this to give realistic results, one would want a very detailed sector classification, preferably with alternative (or, at least, the best) techniques. With such a detailed sector classification, the type of make, buy or sell decisions we are after would appear more appropriate.[1] In the present classification, many of the sectors are indeed sufficiently homogeneous to make sense of the solution. Thus rice, jute, tea, sugar, cigarettes, cotton textiles, jute textiles, paper and cement are fairly homogeneous tradeable sectors for which the recommended solutions are reasonably unambiguous. Sectors like other agriculture, edible oils, other food, other textiles, chemicals, basic metals, machinery, transport equipment and miscellaneous manufactures are very heterogeneous, however. It would usually be wrong to assume that the model recommendation would apply to all products within such a sector. Ideally, it would be desirable to disaggregate optimally. Since this has not been possible, we might try to make the best use of the available results until better applications are made, by combining it with additional information.

---

[1] The model does not require that every sector be either produced or imported. If π is the same as import cost, both may be done. We did get some results of this kind for some sectors.

Thus, to decide whether a particular chemical should be produced or not, we might ask to what extent its production structure, import cost, etc. resemble the average chemicals sector in the model. If it is fairly similar, there would be little compelling reason to change the decision. If it is very different, the accounting prices of the model, suitably adjusted by the relevant border price information, might be used to evaluate its profitability.

The same procedure ought to apply if there is any strong reason to believe that the incremental production structure of a sector is going to be much different from the average. In general no output expansion should be allowed for the socially low profit sectors like sugar, cigarettes and paper unless it can be argued that the production structure of the incremental output would be vastly different and that such a difference is likely to reduce the accounting cost of production.

Our second point relates to the fact that some sectors which are quite unambiguously identified as unprofitable have quite a bit of existing capacity. Examples are sugar, cigarettes and paper. The model tells us not to expand their capacities but neither does it quite tell us to scrap the existing capacity. Because of incorrect incentives and policies in the past, capacities have been created for these sectors whose scrap value would probably be very little. To find out whether the existing capacities ought to be utilised, one should re-evaluate the profitability of these sectors on the assumption that the capital cost of existing output is no more than the replacement requirement and scrap value of the existing capital stock. Given the preponderance of the interest cost on capital of some of these sectors (e.g. paper, which is one of the most capital-intensive industries in Bangladesh) it is very likely that the continued utilisation of the existing capacity will turn out to be profitable.

11 Agriculture and Land Reform

11.1 A CHANGE IN DIRECTION

OUR discussion in the earlier chapters emphasised the past discrimination against agriculture. Such discrimination was carried through by means of heavy 'concealed taxation' of agriculture, by keeping the incentives low and by providing little public sector investment. The result was stagnation and decline. The rate of growth of this massive sector being small in aggregate terms and negative in per capita terms, the overall growth for the economy had a strong downward pull. Large grain deficits became a regular feature making heavy demand on foreign exchange. Export of agricultural goods (predominantly jute) suffered as a result of negative policies. The policy of maximising short-term gain by using monopoly power over the supply of jute subjected this vital export crop to long-term uncertainties of competition from synthetics.

There was little justification for such policies from the standpoint of maximising social gain. All the agricultural activities specified in the model in Chapter 10 are socially as profitable as any. And this is not due to any systematic bias arising out of any underenumeration of the incremental cost. In the model such costs have been carefully based on what might be the input requirements at the margin and are considerably higher than the low average costs. Unlike the usual kinds of multisectoral models, we made allowance for the cost of land. Finally, the fairly high shadow wage *ratio* means that the favourable outcome of the model for agriculture is not due primarily to its relative labour intensity.

The lines of future expansion are rather clearly indicated. To wipe out the existing grain deficit and the varying degree of starvation suffered by nearly half of the population are of very high priority. Raw jute price in terms of foreign exchange will have to be lowered and in terms of domestic currency raised. Since the very large premium accruing previously to the (West) Pakistani owners of jute textile mills and the traders who acquired import entitlements against the foreign exchange earned by jute would now be available to finance these changes, there would be no need for a government subsidy; in fact, the Government may be able to end up with a bit of the margin in its own exchequer. Demand for jute is likely to increase in the manufacturing countries abroad as a result of these changes in policy. More important, it should be possible to persuade India to give up some or most of her raw jute cultivation for cheaper jute from Bangladesh. At the very least, India would satisfy her incremental demand for jute from Bangladesh. Thus jute output is due for a jump. The third major expansion in the short run would consist of import substitution of oilseeds, a good deal of which used to be imported from (West) Pakistan.

In the longer run, agricultural production will have to adapt to the needs of better quality of food by emphasising livestock, poultry and fishery. It is quite clear that both in the short and in the long run, agriculture can profitably absorb quite a large quantity of resources. The questions are: (*a*) under what institutional structure will such growth be promoted?; (*b*) how will agriculture ,with so little saving and internal capital formation in the past, be induced to undertake the high rate of investment that would be involved?; and (*c*) what technical form will investment take? It will be futile to try to provide complete answers to all these questions. Our purpose in this chapter is merely to explore the possibilities in some of the directions indicated by these questions.

11.2 LAND REFORM

11.2.1 *The context*

It has often been suggested that the enthusiasm for land reform and that for industrialisation are contradictory. The idea derives from the widely observed phenomenon that land reform pushes a much greater proportion of agriculture into the area of subsistence activities, thereby reducing both investible and marketable surpluses. Historically, the argument has been found to contain a good deal of truth and the *ex post* justification for land reform in many cases could only be found in the greater emphasis on the principle of equity as compared to that for efficiency. Much of the force of such an argument would, however, appear to be lost in the case of Bangladesh today and this would appear to be due to the fact that the present question of land reform in Bangladesh is very different from the standard classical models.

At the risk of oversimplification, one might classify land reforms into two very broad types. The first type of land reform takes place during the transition from feudalism to industrial capitalism and has as its main features the abolition or serious curtailment of the big feudal lords and the distribution of ownership rights to a large number of peasants. The second type of land reform takes place during the transformation of the society from capitalism to socialism and is characterised by the abolition of the private ownership of land. Needless to say, an infinite variation of the two basic kinds can be observed.

The peculiarity of the question of land reform in Bangladesh derives from its being somewhere between the two kinds described above. The first kind of land reform would appear to have taken place in the fifties, although it did not produce the expected result of material progress of agriculture. The second type of land reform is not on the cards. Bangladesh has achieved independence through a nationalist movement whose leadership is claiming a socialist mantle though it is quite clear that their aspirations and methods are typically social democratic. The abolition of the private ownership of land and its substitution by collectivisation is not a programme that would be endorsed by this Government. Nor is it likely that there would be a spontaneous upsurge in the countryside in favour of collectivisation. As we have noted before, the landless households form a very small proportion of the rural population. Despite extreme and widely shared poverty, the vast majority (perhaps no less than 90 per cent) own at least a bit of land. It is not likely to be easy to convince a land-owning peasant, however poor he is and however small his holding may be, that the way to his wellbeing lies through his renunciation of the ownership of land. Thus the question of land reform facing Bangladesh is a unique one. It cannot take the form of redistributing the surplus land of the big landlords among the landless, leaving the middle peasants untouched. The reason simply is that the big landlords do not exist any more and unless parts of the holdings of those who in the classical context would be regarded as middle peasants are subjected to acquisition, no significant redistribubutable surplus of land would emerge.

11.2.2 *Efficiency and farm size*

If the first kind of land reform has already taken place and the conditions for the other kind do not exist, why is it at all urgent to have land reform? Part of the urgency derives from political and distributional considerations. The political slogan of land redistribution has appealed to the majority of the farmers who have very little or no land. During the recent political struggle, many of them developed expectations of some kind of redistribution of ownership. With the average farm size of 2½ acres and about a third of the agricultural households with less than an acre or nothing at all, the existence of ownership units of more than 30 acres at the other tail of the distribution would appear to indicate an intolerable degree of inequality.

There are also strong economic arguments. Under the 1950 reform, the agriculture of Bangladesh could not achieve material progress at any reasonable rate. The bigger farmers after the reform were big enough to feel themselves a part of the rural gentry, thereby avoiding farming both as a manual and as an entrepreneurial activity and imposing on agriculture serious costs in the form of high consumption, absenteeism and the institution of sharecropping. But they were not big enough or motivated enough (admittedly, given the rather disincentive-creating policies followed by the Government) to generate sufficient surplus to organise farming along capitalist lines and contribute to the increase in agricultural output. As we have noted in Chapter 5, the bigger ownership units have a greater tendency to resort to sharecropping. If sharecropping is the best entrepreneurship they can provide, there would be little justification for perpetuating the existing inequality of ownership distribution.

Another consideration derives from the finding of a large number of surveys in Bangladesh and elsewhere that the employment of labourers per unit of land is a rather sharply decreasing function of the size of the farm. There has been a great deal of discussion to explain the phenomenon. The most plausible explanation seems to be that the smaller farms are more often based entirely on family labour which is plentiful in relation to the size of the farm. Since such labour frequently has little alternative price in the market, the tendency is to employ them on land up to the very maximum, as long as 'the marginal product of labour is positive', to use the economists' standard jargon, until all family labour is used up. For the family farms having an excessive amount of labour supply relative to their size, there will be work-sharing of some sort for quite a range beyond the point of full use of labour (i.e. beyond the point where the marginal product of a man-hour is zero) and visible employment would be even greater than effective employment.

The bigger farms would, on the other hand, depend more on hired labour partly because the farms are too big for the supply of family labour and partly because most of the big farmers would not involve themselves in manual work. They would therefore restrict employment to the level at which marginal yield is the same as market wage (which, despite the excess supply of labour, is not only positive but fairly close to the average standard of living of the poorer farmers). Employment per acre as a consequence will be less than for the family farms. Moreover, there will be little work-sharing so that much of the unemployment will be visible.

We have pointed out earlier the overwhelming problem of unemployment that Bangladesh will be facing. Simply to absorb the addition to the labour force resulting from demographic forces an estimated 0·75 million jobs would have to be created per year in the immediate future. This would use up about 18 per cent of GDP under favourable but conventional technological assumptions. Thus to be able to tackle the problem of employment creation, it is of great importance that flooding of the labour market through the increased proletarianisation of the peasants is avoided. Such proletarianisation must have been taking place in the recent past even if only as a result of demographic factors. To compensate, a redistribution of ownership seems highly desirable so that a greater proportion of farms can be entirely family-based, raising both visible and effective employment in agriculture.

The ownership ceiling is already quite low by the standards of the first kind of land reform discussed above. If any impact is to be created by way of the redistribution of land, it will have to be further reduced rather drastically.

A major argument that is usually made against such a policy of eliminating the larger units is that this leads to a reduction in farm efficiency and agricultural productivity. We would like to argue that at least in the context of Bangladesh agriculture, there would be little validity for such conclusions. For this purpose, we find it useful to distinguish between static and dynamic efficiency, the former referring to productivity per acre under the assumption that *technology does not change* and the latter to the rate of adoption of *improved technology*.

As far as static efficiency goes, the weight of evidence seems to suggest the exact opposite of the above contention. By now quite a large number of surveys are available to show that *output per acre* is larger for the smaller farms while *profit per acre* (valuing all inputs at market costs) may be higher for the larger farms. Such results have been obtained in repeated and independent surveys in Bangladesh, India, Ceylon and other countries.[1] The explanation almost certainly lies in the phenomenon already discussed, that the smaller farms, based more often entirely on family labour, would push employment to the point of zero marginal productivity (point N_s in the diagram) while the larger farms, hiring labour at the going wage rate (W_o), restrict employment by equating marginal productivity with the wage rate (to the point N_l in the diagram). Thus labour input per unit of land will be N_l for the large farms and N_s for the small farms. Since the marginal product of labour in the range between them is still positive, output per acre would

[1] The results for Bangladesh are based on the surveys conducted by the Dacca University Bureau of Economic Research and the Bangladesh Institute of Development Economics. The result of the former was reported by M. Habibullah at the Annual Conference of the Pakistan Economic Association in 1968 and published in the 1968 Conference Issue of the *Pakistan Economic Journal*. Indian surveys have been widely discussed. Pioneered by A. K. Sen, a considerable amount of controversy was published in the *Economic Weekly* during 1963 and 1964. The Ceylonese result is based on a Central Bank survey analysed by K. B. Griffin, *Economic Aspects of Technical Change in the Rural Areas of Monsoon Asia* (UNRISD, Geneva, January 1972).

be higher for the smaller farms than for the bigger farms (by the amount of the curvilinear triangle $N_l N_s q$).[1] By now the evidence is so overwhelming that it seems quite unnecessary to worry that the exact opposite may be true.

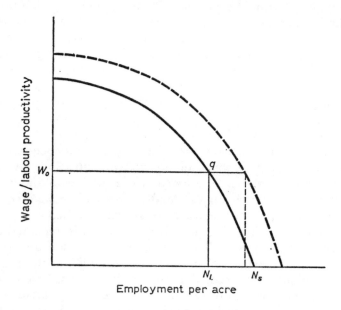

Employment per acre

There, however, seem to exist *a priori* arguments that the dynamic efficiency would be greater for the larger farms. First, their bigger size would mean better scope for the efficient use of modern inputs; irrigation, pesticides, and even machines. They should also have a larger investible surplus per acre and greater creditworthiness to borrow to incorporate modern technology. In other words, they should be better able to bring about a shift in the marginal productivity curve (shown by the dotted line in the diagram) so that what is lost by employment restriction will be more than offset by the introduction of a better technology.

Whatever the strength of the *a priori* argument, facts do not corroborate it for Bangladesh. The bigger farms have not shown any significant tendency to modernise. In fact, our evidence suggests that the bigger farms are more often associated with

---

[1] See A. K. Sen, op. cit., for the original statement of the argument.

inefficient institutions like sharecropping. While a smaller farmer has no alternative but to squeeze out a living from land by working on it himself, a bigger owner, both because his past wellbeing has perhaps enabled him to have other sources of income and because his larger holding of land is enough to assure him a reasonable living even if it is rented out, would more often be tempted to have his land sharecropped.

No doubt the bigger farmers could get higher profits if they provided the entrepreneurship and investment themselves, particularly in view of their better creditworthiness and knowledge, but they preferred to do what they did. The explanation may partly lie in sociological factors like the motivation of the traditional families. It may also have been due to the fact that although very large in relation to the average farm size, the bigger farms have not been big enough to generate sufficient surplus and seize the opportunity of dynamic growth, particularly in view of the government policy of disincentives of various kinds.[1]

Now that we are arguing for a much more helpful government attitude towards agriculture, would it make sense to allow the bigger farmers to continue to exist? To justify anything like this, one must argue that the bigger farms would be better able to take advantage of direct government assistance. Even if this were true, there would be strong arguments against their continuation. A government assistance programme may indeed raise the profitability of the bigger farms more than that of the smaller ones and thereby create serious problems. If no restraint is put on size, the effect of such assistance will be to increase the ability of the larger farms to swallow up the smaller ones. Increased proletarianisation of the peasants will follow with the consequent pressure on the economy to cope with the higher number of unemployed. The social, political and economic consequences of such policies may be quite disastrous. It would seem much more sensible to make the extra public sector effort that might be needed to make up for the non-existence of the

[1] Far be it from the author to suggest that this points to the need for increasing the size of the bigger farms even more. In the given land/man ratio obtaining in Bangladesh and the likely continuation of the imbalance between labour supply and demand in non-agricultural sectors, such a policy would have no sensible basis.

big farms or even to tolerate slightly lower output in order to avoid such consequences.

It is, however, far from certain that such additional effort or sacrifice of output would be necessary. Much of the arguments for the greater ability of the larger farms to take advantage of the helping hand stretched out by the government would appear to be based on uncertain foundations. The bigger ownership unit rarely means bigger consolidated operating unit. As we have seen in Chapter 5 above, 97 per cent of the bigger farms are fragmented, often into ten plots each. Thus the argument of economies of scale in farming hardly has any relevance. Nor does it seem to be a particularly easy task to consolidate the holdings without very considerable redistribution.

The argument that the marginal rate of saving would be higher for the larger farms appears more plausible on *a priori* grounds, but there is also the likelihood that the greater mobility and urban contact of the larger farmers will make them higher consumers. We have little empirical evidence to allow us to judge which of the factors might predominate. Finally, it may be important to remember that a good deal of evidence exists for similar cases to indicate the possibility of raising the marginal saving rate of the smaller farmers by making investment packages sufficiently divisible and obtaining other appropriate policies.

11.2.3 *Criteria for the ceiling on holdings*

The very first question to be settled about land reform is the ceiling on ownership. We have argued above that on grounds of static efficiency it may be distinctly advantageous to split up the bigger farms into smaller units.[1] About dynamic efficiency in the context of adopting a better technology we are less sure, but would tend to believe that increased government assistance to agriculture without a lower ceiling on ownership is likely to encourage a bi-modal kind of development leading to the increased proletarianisation of the small peasants.

[1] The argument is about the consequence of splitting the farms that are so big that family labour is inadequate for their operation and thus they become dependent on the hiring of labour. It should not be interpreted to mean that the very small farms can be made more efficient by splitting them into even smaller sizes.

One of the major objectives of redistribution should be to raise the size of the tiny farms from a fraction of an acre to a more reasonable size. This would be a source of increased efficiency provided by land reform. Another objective should be to attain some consolidation of holdings. By emphasising this objective, the average size of the operating units could easily be raised while the absolute limit of the ownership units is brought down rather drastically. Abolition of disincentive systems such as sharecropping might be yet another objective. Within the framework of these efficiency-promoting objectives a more equitable distribution of land ownership must dominate.

To get some idea of the magnitude of the problem, it may be useful to refer to some numerical illustrations. Today roughly 4 million farms have holdings below 2½ acres;[1] their average holding is only 1·19 acres. A million farms are less than half an acre and, perhaps, hundreds of thousands are below a tenth of an acre. It is inconceivable that much farming activity goes on on these tiny bits of land euphemistically categorised as farms. Suppose we want to raise the average size of these 4 million farms to 2 acres. The amount of 'surplus' land that must be taken over from the larger farms to achieve this modest objective would be about 3¼ million acres. To generate the indicated amount of surplus land, the ceiling on ownership will have to be fixed at about 6½ acres.

Table 11.1 shows some estimates of surplus land for alternative ceilings. The estimates are based on the frequency distributions of farms and land area according to ownership units derived in 1967/68. Even among these above-average-sized farms, there may have been a general decline in size due to the inexorable forces of inheritance under Islamic law during a period over which rural population increased significantly. Thus our estimates may easily have been too high.

What the estimates show, however, is that even if the ceiling is drastically reduced to 5 acres, the surplus land will be just over 5 million acres, or just enough to bring the average size of the holdings of the smallest 64 per cent of farms up to 2·5 acres! But 5 acres will be an unrealistically low ceiling. Resistance to it would be strong, as nearly a fifth of all farmers would stand to lose some land. A ceiling of 7·5 acres, which

[1] This is obtained from the 1968 Master Survey.

may be somewhat more feasible in view of the fact that only 8 per cent of the farmers would be affected, will generate only 2·6 million acres of surplus land with which little more can be achieved than bringing up to 1·5-acre size all farms which are below it. With a ceiling of 10 or 12·5 acres, the surplus land generated would hardly create a big impact by way of redistribution.

TABLE 11.1

ESTIMATES OF 'SURPLUS' LAND FOR SOME
ALTERNATIVE CEILINGS ON OWNERSHIP

Ceiling at (acres)	Surplus land (million acres)
5	5·21
7·5	2·63
10	1·65
12·5	1·09

NOTE
We have used the actual frequency distribution from the 1968 Master Survey of Agriculture.

Several facts stand out. First, in order to create a major impact, it would be necessary to reduce the ceiling drastically; anything significantly above 7·5 acres[1] would provide little opportunity to create a major impact in terms of redistribution. Secondly, even with such a drastically low ceiling, it will be impossible to bring up the smallest few million farms to any reasonable size. To try to distribute land among the landless households would be impossible.[2] The arithmetic merely quan-

[1] We are limited to these discrete figures since the frequency distributions are available only for these groups.

[2] It is not being suggested that the landless should not get any land. It will be an impossibly tricky job to decide who should get land, the landless or those who have below average holdings. While equity would dictate a preference for the former, efficiency would dictate a preference for the latter. Actual decision must be based on a careful balancing of these objectives.

tifies what should be obvious to anyone aware of the extremely low overall land/man ratio: even if the land redistribution programme aims at the kind of upper ceiling unknown in the conventional land reforms carried out in the past, millions of farms would remain too small to provide either a subsistence income or a reasonable degree of farming efficiency[1] and hundreds of thousands of households would continue to be without any land.

What would be the consequences of a $7\frac{1}{2}$-acre or even a 5-acre limit on ownership on farming efficiency and agricultural productivity? Mechanisation is the only process that would encounter a serious obstacle. Unless many farms can be put together into some kind of collective effort, it will not pay to use tractors and harvesters. In the excess labour supply situation of Bangladesh, one perhaps need not worry about the technical economies of scale of a technology which on purely economic calculations will remain socially unprofitable in the foreseeable future.

The other modern technique that may appear to have difficulty would be winter irrigation, through tubewells and low-lift pumps. There will be no way to utilise efficiently a *private* tubewell or pump. The efficient use of a very small low-lift pump or tubewell of 1 cusec capacity would require a minimum land area of 25 acres, perhaps very much more in the case of the tubewell. Thus even under the existing land ownership pattern, no significant proportion of total acreage will qualify for private enterprise in this line. About $4\frac{1}{2}$ per cent of total acreage is held in ownership units of more than 25 acres, but 97 per cent of such ownership units are fragmented into an average of four or five plots per owner. It is no wonder that all the irrigation provided through such means have been made available by public sector authorities.

The other types of modern technology, e.g. improved seed, fertiliser and pest control, can be used just as efficiently on a 5-acre farm as on a 30-acre one. Types of pest control operation like aerial spraying will have significant economies of scale but only beyond the maximum size of all the farms in

---

[1] This is not a contradiction. Although a large farm may be less efficient than a small farm of a reasonable size, a farm of a fraction of an acre will certainly be less efficient than a small farm of more reasonable size, say two acres.

Bangladesh today. What little of such services is available is provided by the public sector.

We have argued above that while it is conceivable that the marginal saving rates would be higher for the bigger farms, neither *a priori* reasoning nor empirical evidence suggests any unambiguous or overwhelming advantage for them on this count. On the other hand, it should be possible to get the larger number of medium and smaller farms to save a reasonable proportion of their incremental outputs once the improved technology is made available to them in sufficiently divisible units.

Land reform will contribute to the increased efficiency of farming in several ways. First, much of sharecropping will be eliminated even if no statutory abolition is resorted to. This is because landowners who hope to live largely on the income from land sharecropped by others have to have a much larger unit of ownership than would be permitted by the ceiling. Again, a positive effect on productivity could result from the increase in the size of the many tiny farms. Careful planning of the redistribution programme should allow a significant consolidation of holdings in spite of the drastic reduction in the ceiling on ownership. Once again, in the context of monsoon rice agriculture of Bangladesh, fragmentation of holdings seems to be less of an obstacle than is usually supposed. Rice cultivation requires a good deal of fragmentation of land into small plots surrounded by low dykes. The main advantage of consolidation lies in the savings of labour and the convenience of mechanisation which are important considerations for the maximisation of profit under capitalist agriculture, but hardly of any great importance for the labour-abundant peasant agriculture of Bangladesh.

11.2.4 *Implementing land reform*

Since the prospective recipients of surplus land would all be very small farmers and landless workers, there would be few who could finance the purchase of land from past savings or market borrowings. Inevitably, payments will have to be staggered over a number of years to be paid out of savings made from future outputs. Special credit might be provided for this purpose through the setting up of a Land Bank which would act as the intermediary between the recipients and past owners of land.

Even if the ceiling on ownership is as low as 7½ acres, only a fraction of the qualified recipients could be given land unless one wanted to distribute the surplus land very thinly. Since not all demand can be met, there must be some device for rationing. This could be done either through administrative decisions or through the market. Each of these mechanisms has difficulties. Administrative decisions are apt to be arbitrary. It is not easy to define the priorities in a situation of large excess demand. Even if the priorities are defined somehow, their successful implementation would depend on the existence of an efficient and incorruptible administrative organisation. Such an organisation is not available at this moment. On the other hand, the market would inevitably distribute land among the richer farmers who would outbid the poorer ones.

The way out may be to allow the forces of the market to operate within the framework of clearly defined priorities, such as the exclusion of the bigger than average farmers from bidding and the designing of the credit programme of the Land Bank to reduce the disabilities of the groups that are at a disadvantage. Thus the relative weakness of the landless can be offset to a considerable extent if the payment is to be made out of the future yield and if priority is assigned to them in the distribution of the Land Bank credit.

Once the price is settled in the market, the payment can be staggered over a maximum number of years in such a way that the aggregate annual payment remains less than it would be under sharecropping. A typical scheme may be to spread the payment over fifteen equal annual instalments when the price in the market is five times the average annual yield, at the rate of a third of standard annual output. The usual sharecropping arrangement is to pay the landlord half the gross output. To do away with the disincentive of high proportional taxation that sharecropping is, the payments (i.e. the price of land) should be fixed and not tied to actual yield.

In view of the increased public sector participation in agricultural investment and the need to finance it, it should be desirable to keep the payment of compensation to the former landlords lower than the receipt from the recipients of land.

The scheme will then amount to a compulsory order on the owners of more than 7½ acres to sell the surplus land over and above the limit in the market from which the bigger than average farmers are excluded under a specified system of payment through a Land Bank and subject to a moderate rate of sales tax.

Even if the above blueprint is implemented, absentee ownership will continue to exist. Such arrangements will lead to sharecropping, cash renting and similar practices. In view of the increased general inefficiency of these, there does not seem to be any case for the continued existence of absentee ownership. Unless statutory provisions are made to abolish this practice, the fixing of the ownership ceiling will almost certainly encourage the increased resort to this loophole. It would, therefore, be necessary to require physical participation in the major operations of the production process as a necessary condition of land ownership. Admittedly, this will eliminate entrepreneurship in agriculture as an activity independent of and separate from labour. Such entrepreneurship is often considered by agricultural economists to be the driving force behind capitalist farming. However profitable it might be, in the context of the extremely unfavourable land/man ratio obtaining in Bangladesh, the attempt to foster agricultural growth through the promotion of capitalist farming will lead to intolerable stresses. Nor will the ceiling of 7½ acres (or anything else that is practicable for more than a very few farms in view of the extreme land shortage) provide much scope for capitalist farming. It therefore seems sensible to opt fully for the peasant family farm rather than to allow some of the inefficient features of capitalist farming to coexist with them.

We have argued that a drastic reduction in ownership limit will on balance be both equitable and efficient. Also, this would be the only way of having agricultural growth without an increased proletarianisation of the peasants. It would, on the other hand, be naïve to pretend that the kind of reform outlined above can be achieved easily. The reforms will mean drastic change in the rural social structure. They will mean the complete abolition of the rural gentry, people who may not on the average have as high standards of living as those of the feudal classes in other countries but who survive on the perpetuation of inefficient tenure systems contributing to the general stagnation of agriculture. Around them revolves the local social and political power structure in rural Bangladesh. It is inconceivable that this entire class will submit to annihilation without putting up a fight. Nor are the prospects improved by the amazing lack of a sense of urgency and of the seriousness of the problem among the organised political parties.[1]

11.3 PUBLIC SECTOR AND AGRICULTURAL POLICY

Our discussion of the remainder of agricultural policy can be brief since it is neither our purpose nor within our competence to deal with the many details of technical and institutional planning. Even with the existing distribution of land ownership, it was too much to hope that the farmers of Bangladesh will have enough dynamism and saving capacity to adopt the newer and better production techniques. The reasons are many: too few of them are big enough to generate sufficient internal saving to finance any reasonable capital investment; too many of them are just big enough to be on the margin of inefficiency in which sharecropping and other kinds of semi-absenteeism flourish; there were strong disincentives in the form of unfavourable terms of trade both internal and external; the supply of credit

[1] The symptom is fully expressed in the stand taken by the Bangladesh Communist Party (the one led by Moni Singh, usually identified as the 'pro-Moscow' group and probably the best organised of the Marxist parties). In its programme for the National Liberation Front (to consist of themselves and the other patriotic groups, including the Awami League), adopted as recently as 22 May 1971, they propose 'the ceiling on ownership of land to be fixed at 100 bighas (33·3 acres) per family and the surplus land to be distributed free among the poor and landless peasants according to priorities. To compensate adequately the landlords whose land will be taken over by the Government.' See the Party pamphlet (in Bengali, *Bangladesher Shadhinota Sangramer Mullayan*), *The Evaluation of the Freedom Struggle of Bangladesh* [translation and the figure in parenthesis by the author]. The ceiling of 33·3 acres will generate almost no redistributable surplus. The principle of free distribution is inconsistent with that of full compensation if the programme is to be anything but marginal. When the position of the most organised and vocal party of the far left is so sadly inadequate a reflection of the realities, it can be imagined how the more moderate parties would react. One is tempted to conclude that the 93 per cent of the Bengalis who live in rural Bangladesh have received altogether too little attention not only from the past regimes but also in the thinking of those who have been fighting for change.

was inelastic and expensive; there was too little government investment to reduce the serious uncertainties of flooding and other natural disasters and there has been negligible public sector participation in providing extension and other modern inputs.

The question of incentive, particularly with respect to raw jute, has been discussed above at great length. The adjustment of the exchange rate through a devaluation of about 64 per cent immediately after independence would have proved helpful had not much of it been neutralised by an export tax on jute. The policy for the long-term rate of exchange for jute is rather crucial and must be based on a reappraisal of what is a hangover from the past. From a practical point of view, the export tax on raw jute will only encourage smuggling across the border, which will be far more free now than ever before.

The price policy for food grains must also be handled with great care. There will at times be intense pressure to supply grains at low prices. It will, however, be futile to try to solve the problem of poverty and income distribution with measures of price and distribution control which can at best handle short-term and transitory problems. We have enough experience from the past of the effect of policies like compulsory procurement at low prices in aggravating the basic problem of low output. One of the effects of the opening up of trade with India means that the Bangladesh economy will have to adjust closer to the relative prices of its giant neighbour. The huge border that would be impossible to police will otherwise ensure this through illegal trading. Bangladesh will have to be reconciled with higher food prices as a result. More will be said on this in the final chapter.

The crucial role of public sector organisations in providing extension and even some entrepreneurship in the situation of small peasant farming has been underlined before. A modest programme was mounted in the past through the Thana Irrigation Project (TIP)[1] under which a package of inputs (water from low-lift pump, fertiliser and often improved seed) was provided against short-term credit at a reasonable rate of interest. The weaknesses of the programme were many: the extension service was poor and inadequate; the credit in kind followed too rigid a

[1] Thana is the lowest administrative unit in Bangladesh and consists of a police station (which is the literal translation of the word *Thana*).

ratio among various inputs; experimental seed varieties were pushed with great enthusiasm, leading to disastrous consequences at times; although the programme was carried out under the banner of the co-operative, its administration and control were bureaucratic. The main programme was aimed at increasing winter acreage and as far as it can go it might be quite a sensible thing to do. But it appears that the principal motivation behind the programme was the intent to postpone the massive investment in flood control without which rainy season crops were faced with serious bottlenecks. It was perhaps hoped that by extending winter acreage. the small boro crop of the time could be made the biggest rice crop, thereby eliminating the deficit. As a result little attention was paid to the two main rice crops during the rainy season.

The programme should be increased greatly and extended over all the major crops in all the major seasons. There does not seem to be a great prospect of introducing modern inputs in the peasant-ownership agriculture of Bangladesh unless they are initially provided by the Government with adequate backing of short-term credit and extension services. We do not intend to go into very many details, but it seems worthwhile to discuss a few principles of organising such a programme.

First, a great deal of care must be taken in deciding the technologies which deserve to be introduced. In the past, there was too little applied research in botanical-genetical aspects of seed development. Past input programmes were extremely rigid and based on complete distrust of the peasants' motives and abilities. To illustrate, the TIP distributed credit in kind with a rigidly fixed proportion between fertiliser and acreage for the whole country. It was doubtful whether the quantities were economically optimal. At more than 800 lbs per acre (for IRRI rice) it was thought by many to be too high, perhaps rightly so in view of the high urea content. Even if this were the right dose when all other inputs are in right proportion, it would not be so if the farmers were unable to provide the complementary inputs. Instead of taking the farmer into its confidence and trying to educate him through a proper extension service, the TIP resorted to distributing a fixed quantity of fertiliser per acre to all applicants for credit. It is believed that many farmers sold part of the fertiliser thus received to reconvert their credit into cash.

Since fertiliser could openly be bought at a fixed price, the sale in this kind of 'black market' was carried out at a price less than what the farmer paid the TIP, thereby raising the effective rate of interest on his loan.[1] It would make much better sense to let the farmer decide about the composition of his borrowing in kind while trying to educate him through extension programmes. At the very least, a good deal of flexibility among the ratios of various inputs in kind ought to be introduced.

The next principle to emphasise is that although it would be desirable to help remove the disability of the farmers by the provision of credit and inputs at reasonable prices, there would be little reason to think that agricultural progress will be helped by the underpricing of inputs. First, underpricing should be unnecessary if the inputs programme is a sensible one. The return on modern inputs is very high by all accounts and there should be no problem in repaying the credit in a few months' time. In special cases and during serious crop failures some re-scheduling of credit may be necessary. But, on the average, the inputs should not only be able to pay for themselves but also ensure high profits to the farmer. Secondly, with a massive input programme, any significant underpricing will be difficult to finance. Finally, pricing any input below its social cost will lead to the well-known phenomenon of its wasteful use.

The problem of credit is of crucial importance since much of the modern inputs programme will have to be backed by such credit. If the farmers are taken to be the best judges of their credit requirement, then in the recent past such need would appear to have been in the neighbourhood of Rs. 1200 million.[2] This would be about 8 per cent of GDP originating in agriculture or just over 4 per cent of total GDP. This is indeed a large sum, but by no means beyond the ability of the Government to finance. Just to get a feeling of the order of magnitude involved, the amount is within the projected revenue surplus of the Government. Also it is very much a once-for-all operation since

[1] The author's attention to this allegedly widespread phenomenon was drawn by the Registrar of the Co-operative Societies, the department which administered the programme.

[2] This is based on the finding of the 1966 Credit Survey that 46 per cent of all farm households needed credit of Rs. 309 per year on the average.

the credit need is short-term, circulating on the average more than once a year. It would even make sense to borrow for this purpose from abroad.

Why is it that the Government, which in the recent past supplied only 14 per cent of the credit available (and about 5 per cent of what was needed) will in future have to supply *all* credit? For one thing, we are not quite certain that this will be the case, although there are strong reasons for believing that the Government and institutional sources would have to provide *most* of the credit. In fact, net credit from private sources may have been negligible even in the past. Although no direct measurements are available, it appears from all the many rudimentary sources that the rate of interest on such non-institutional borrowing has been very high. Frequently, after years of interest payment at a very high effective rate, the borrower ends up losing the mortgaged land. There is every reason to believe that the annual rate of growth in the farmers' indebtedness to these sources has been lower than the effective rate of interest, implying a negative rate of *net* credit inflow. To end the continued exploitation of the small peasants by these moneylenders (euphemistically called 'rural well-to-do' by the 1966 Credit Survey), it would be necessary to go into the history of these contracts to decide whether they ought to be repudiated or not.

Besides participation in getting the peasant farmers to transform their farming by the adoption of more productive techniques, the public sector will also have to bear responsibility for developing some of the infrastructural facilities. Feeder transport, marketing organisation and storage facilities have always been inadequate and will become real bottlenecks once there is a discontinuous jump in output. Careful provision for the expansion of these facilities must be planned ahead of demand. The most important area of overhead investment will, however, be flood control, to which we now turn our attention.

11.4 THE STRATEGY OF FLOOD CONTROL

In our discussion in Chapter 7, we noted that the very first step in this direction, involving the preparation of a technical feasibility study, had not been taken. Thus the first thing to be done is to decide the technical solution from a consideration of the alternatives. The circumstances of independence should make it possible to look into the alternative of doing so in co-operation with the most important upper riparian country, India. Until such studies are available, one would be confined within the region of speculation in trying to estimate the cost and the possibility of finance. It may, however, be useful to point out some specific considerations which ought to be recognised.

Over the last decade, the central Pakistan Government had systematically spread the doctrine that flood control is a massive investment project which is beyond the means of the country's internal resources and could only be undertaken with a great deal of external assistance. While the doctrine contained some elements of truth, it also spread many seriously mistaken ideas.

To protect fifteen million acres from potential flooding is indeed a massive job and will require very large, though still unspecified, quantities of resources. But the one important consideration that is usually not taken into account is that the input that is required most, human labour, is plentifully available in Bangladesh.

Fixed capital requirement per unit of conventional construction output is very low. In the kind of construction that is likely to be involved in flood control—embankments, canals and earth-moving works in general – technologies which use labour even more intensively would be available and would prove efficient for the relative resource endowment of Bangladesh. Physical capital requirement would be a small fraction of the value of construction involved if the appropriate technology is used. In formulating the technical blueprint for flood control, this fundamental fact of the relative factor endowment should be taken into account.[1]

Thus a large part of the flood control project may be looked upon as an exercise in utilising on an astronomical scale the vast reservoir of human labour. A good deal of it may be possible to

[1] Those who are sceptical about what bare hands and little else can achieve have often been reminded of the Pyramids, the magnificent railway tunnels in Europe and similar other things. A more recent and appropriate example is the millions of *mous* of land reclaimed lately in China.

achieve without much real investment at all, merely through good and imaginative extension work. It should be possible to identify the local segments of the master plan which for a given continuous area will have no significant external economy and mobilise local voluntary labour to undertake these with the help of equipment (and perhaps some nominal rate of wage) supplied by the flood control authority.

The bigger parts involving externalities will have to be organised by a central authority. But the resources that would be necessary to do so would consist, apart from the very modest proportion of equipment, of wage goods. Given the uncomplicated consumption behaviour of the rural population, most of the additional real cost would be met by the increased supply of rice, wheat, coarse cloth and other minor food items. Since the flood control programme should not be delayed until the country can internally generate a surplus (the capacity to do so itself being dependent on the success of the flood control programme) these goods may have to be bought from abroad. This kind of commodity aid has in the past been relatively easy to negotiate. What is more, such aid has often largely been in the form of a grant with only partial repayment, as in the case of P.L. 480 aid, in domestic currency. It would make sense to try to obtain such assistance specifically for this purpose while carefully ensuring that such inflow of agricultural goods does not distort domestic prices to the extent of affecting the incentives for the domestic production plan.

The flood control programme, thus viewed, is a huge organisational exercise. This is where the demand on a scarce resource comes in. For efficient and incorruptible grass-roots organisation is indeed a very scarce resource. Unless this resource can be generated in the required quantity, the whole programme may easily degenerate into the kind of works programme of the days of authoritarian alien rule involving inefficient technology, operation well within the efficiency frontier and the channelling of resources into political patronage.[1]

That flood control is well worth attempting without any delay has been argued extensively in Part II above. The lost

[1] For an evaluation of the works programme in the past, see Rahman Sobhan, *Basic Democracy and Works Programme* (Bureau of Economic Research, University of Dacca, 1969).

rice crop alone in one year of moderate flooding was estimated to have been 220 million dollars. Counting the loss of livestock, housing and other assets, the figure would be much higher. It does not seem likely that the figure would be a small proportion of the possible cost of flood control.

12 Planning Industrialisation

12.1 LESSONS FROM THE PAST

THE quarter-century of partnership in Pakistan should have taught Bangladesh valuable lessons in industrial policy. The main features of the past industrialisation policy have been discussed in considerable detail in some of the previous chapters. We begin the present one with a brief recapitulation.

The basic tenet of Pakistan's industrialisation policy was development through private enterprise. But this did not mean a policy of relative *laissez-faire* or even selective intervention in the case of externalities, infant industries and other standard considerations. The policy took the form of massive state support to promote private capitalism at the cost of imposing an unfavourable distribution of income and an inefficient allocation of resources on the society. The private capitalists were promoted and protected by the setting up of a mechanism of income transfer from the poorer sectors of the economy, by allowing the perpetuation of an oligopolistic banking system, by underpricing the inputs they used and overpricing the products they sold through the manipulation of the instruments of direct control on trade and economic activity, by the use of public revenue to develop the industries with high initial risk only to transfer them to the private sector once profitability was ensured, by severe discrimination against smaller enterprises and by general obstacles to entry. The justifications were that the private capitalists would save and invest at a high rate and provide entrepreneurship which was very scarce. None of these can be accepted as a convincing *ex post* justification. All calculations show that private capitalists have not been high savers and that their savings might well have been less than the 'net subsidy' they indirectly obtained merely through the underpricing of the import entitlements received by them.[1] The argument of entrepreneurship is also dubious in so far as massive aid to one big

[1] See Nuruddin Chowdhury, 'Income Redistributive Intermediation in Pakistan' in the *Pakistan Development Review*, summer 1969.

entrepreneur in most cases meant a strong disincentive for and the ultimate elimination of many small entrepreneurs. What the country got as a result of all these measures were: a highly inefficient large-scale manufacturing industry which, though extremely profitable to the private capitalists because of the arbitrarily distorted market prices, was of relatively small value to the society (i.e. unprofitable if all valuations are based on relative social scarcities); and a strong disincentive for the small-scale and cottage enterprises (and for agriculture), leading to their stagnation and the consequent unfavourable change in the distribution of income.

The lessons are clear. If the scarcity of entrepreneurial and managerial manpower calls for tolerance of private enterprise, it does not warrant the kind of massive aid there was in the past. Pressures for subsidy through the setting up of some mechanism of transferring income from the poorer sectors, excessively low effective rates of taxes and the distribution of entitlements to underpriced inputs must be resisted. Healthy industrialisation is impossible under the kind of state-sponsored private enterprise that would emerge from these measures.

12.2 PUBLIC AND PRIVATE SECTORS

Because of the circumstances of independence leading to the automatic takeover of the enterprises deserted by the (West) Pakistani owners, none of the 'commanding heights' of the Bangladesh economy are in private hands today. Although the precise extent of it is not known, an incomplete and preliminary estimate suggests that public sector ownership and control extend over more than two-thirds of the large-scale manufacturing industries in terms of the value of assets and employment.[1] Within the biggest decile of these enterprises, public ownership and control are probably complete.

The Bangladesh Government thus suddenly finds itself with

---

[1] About 35 per cent of the 2(j) enterprises are reported to have been deserted by the (West) Pakistani owners, according to an interview with the Industries Minister reported in the *Sunday Times* of 6 Feburary 1972. These enterprises are on the average larger than the average for all the 2(j) enterprises. The BIDC ownership is probably around 30 per cent.

the responsibility of running more than two-thirds of the existing large-scale industries. Thus the very first thing it has to learn is to be able to run these enterprises efficiently. The experience of the Bangladesh (formerly East Pakistan) Industrial Development Corporation will be of use, though its methods are likely to be of little help. Although its enterprises have not been subjected to any *ex post* social cost benefit analysis, there are widespread indications that their efficiency and profitability have been rather low.

With such a large number of enterprises under its management, the Bangladesh Government must work out the criteria of social profitability in as great detail as possible and enforce them. Enterprises must no longer be run along civil service lines. It must be realised that much of the future rate of industrialisation depends on the degree of efficiency and the rate of reinvestment achieved in these industries.

Of course, there is nothing in the declared position of the Government and the political party that runs it to preclude the possibility of transferring the ownership of some or most of these enterprises to the private sector.[1] The two arguments frequently put forward in support of such a policy are: (*a*) that by transferring the enterprises to the private sector, private savings would be mobilised to finance additional public sector investment; and (*b*) that scarce entrepreneurship in the public sector would be conserved and private entrepreneurship encouraged.

The first argument, running very much along the lines used in guiding the EPIDC policy in the past, would appear to contain little substance. It assumes that private enterprise has no profitable investment activity to undertake and would thus contradict the argument of private entrepreneurship which is made in the same breath. We have noted the financially weak position of the private capitalists of Bangladesh. In the past, even collectively they failed to win the bid for the EPIDC

[1] According to its 1970 election programme, the Awami League is committed to nationalise, apart from banking, insurance, arterial transport, foreign trade and jute trade, the following manufacturing industries: 'Heavy industries, including Iron and Steel, Mining, Machine tools, Heavy Engineering, Petrochemicals, Fertiliser, Cement, Fuel and Power'. Note that not one significant enterprise in all these sectors was in private hands in Bangladesh.

enterprises over the (West) Pakistani capitalists. Presumably, they would finance the purchase of the enterprises, if offered, by borrowing from the banking system. Since much of the banking system is already publicly owned while the remainder is due to be nationalised according to the expressed intent of the ruling party, this would then in effect mean that the Government itself would be financing the acquisition of its own assets by the private sector through the provision of credit to be repaid out of future profits. No sensible owner would ever go for such a deal unless he was quite convinced that he would make such a mess of the ownership that abdication was the best way out. The argument that the transfer will help conserve the meagre managerial resources in the public sector is equally unconvincing. Transfer of ownership is not the magic wand that would suddenly generate a supply of managers in the private sector; it will merely mean the transfer of the professional managers from the Government payroll to that of the private capitalists.

On the other hand, the continued public ownership of these enterprises can be a very useful source of surplus for reinvestment in a situation of otherwise low public revenue. Since the enterprises are already in operation, it would make little sense to open up the possibility of at least a part of their profits being channelled into capitalists' consumption, which might, however, be a necessary price to pay for private enterprise when the setting up of a new plant is under consideration.[1]

All our arguments above would be valid only if the Government is able to run these enterprises with reasonable efficiency. Given the extreme scarcity of managerial resources in the country, the task has to be faced with a great deal of determination. In the very short run it might be quite a sensible idea to explore the need to import some managers for a specified short period.

One interesting point to note is that in order to redeem its pledge of nationalisation, the Government does not need to take over any of the existing private manufacturing enterprises (see the preceding footnote). It also appears that the question is

---

[1] The preliminary reports about the nationalisation policy outlined on the first anniversary of the declaration of independence indicate that the Government has indeed opted for the policy of retaining these enterprises under public control.

more or less academic whether the Government nationalises (i.e. declares as a Government monopoly) the future expansion in these sectors. Private capitalists in Bangladesh are in no position to venture into these areas as a competitor of the public sector unless the Government decides to provide them with massive patronage. The crucial decision, therefore, is whether such patronage will be provided or not. In case such patronage is provided, the policy of nationalising a few sectors of the economy will have little meaning. In case the private sector is denied all distorted incentives and left to look after itself, there is little possibility that its resources would be big enough to allow its operation in the very large-scale industries requiring a lot of capital.

12.3 LARGE-SCALE AND SMALL-SCALE INDUSTRIES

In our analysis in Chapter 6, we found that among large-scale, small-scale and cottage enterprises, the small-scale ones have both the highest current output and the highest reinvestible surplus per unit of capital. The comparison was admittedly unsatisfactory due to the differences in the concept and valuation of assets and products and the problem of their comparability among the three groups, but the results were so vastly different as to appear certain to survive the adjustments for these factors.

One thing that needs some clarification is that these small-scale enterprises do not use the traditional techniques of production which are classified under cottage industries. They use a good deal of modern technology and in many cases produce the same goods as do large-scale industries. While a complete analysis of their efficiency must be based on a detailed study of their processes, much of their efficiency in comparison with large-scale enterprises seems to be due to their ability to combine much more labour with a given value of capital and to be able to pay lower wages. The higher labour intensity may partly have been due to the fact that the bigger industrialists had easier access to underpriced capital (both cheaper credit and licensed imports) and to this extent this difference can be removed by equalising incentives in future (although one may wonder whether this would at all be possible if the monopoly capitalists became as dominant as they were in former Pakistan). But almost certainly a part of it is inherent in the very nature of small-scale industries. Large-scale enterprises have many mechanical processes which in small-scale industries are manually or less mechanically operated because the device is not divisible. This is an inherent advantage of a small-scale process in our given relative factor price situation and, though not quantifiable in the absence of more technical information, may be quite substantial.

The other advantage of small-scale industries, that of the ability to pay lower wages, is due partly to their ability to disperse and avoid the concentration to which larger enterprises are often subject. A part of the wage differential between large-scale and small-scale industries may genuinely be due to the real difference in the cost of living, which is higher in concentrated urban conditions.

Compared to the cottage industries, the small-scale ones would again appear to have advantages. This is because a given value of capital seems to be combined with a great deal more labour in cottage activities without any greater output than in small-scale activities. The case seems to be somewhat like operating over that part of an isoquant which is parallel to the axis. The situation is certainly one of work-sharing because of too little capital equipment (which itself may be due to the inadequate supply of crucial raw materials and/or even demand) and a great deal of under-employed labour.

For a very long time cottage industries will remain the residual employment category in manufacturing. They at present 'employ' more than three times the labour force in large and small-scale industries. Whatever their inefficiency compared to the small-scale industries, it would be disastrous to adopt measures to stunt their growth or to starve them of necessary requirements. A proper policy would be to increase the effectiveness of employment in these industries gradually over time. The situation could be improved by raising the ratio of capital to men and by linking the household units with a chain of marketing, raw material supply and credit-providing organisations. The idea would be to approach gradually the efficiency of the small-scale activities. As with agriculture, it would, of course, be unrealistic to expect that this sector can increase or even maintain its share of total employment.

If the evidence compiled in Chapter 6 is even approximately correct, then it would be of special importance to try to obtain expansion of output mainly through the use of small-scale techniques. This would not only ensure that capital is efficiently used but indeed be the only way the employment problem could be approached given the rate of savings that is expected to obtain in the economy. There would, of course, be limitations. Many products are produced only in the large-scale enterprises, although it is uncertain how far this is due to unalterable technological circumstances and how far merely due to techno- logical habits. It would be possible, however, to make a large number of products by small-scale processes. This would be true for textiles, food processing of most kinds, leather goods, print- ing, publishing, metal products and even many types of en- gineering goods. Full advantage of small-scale expansion in these sectors should be taken by removing the disabilities of the small private investors in relation to the large-scale investors.

In the large-scale industries, i.e. the sectors in which either technology or considerations of economies of scale dictate much larger units of enterprise involving the commitment of great quantities of capital, the public sector will have to play the major role. This would in any case be dictated by circumstances; the private capitalists in Bangladesh have command over too little resources to venture into risky and heavy investments. They could, of course, be induced to undertake these activities by introducing massive patronage and distortions in the incentive system, as has been done in the past, but the economic and social consequences of such policies would be entirely negative for the society as a whole.

12.4 SECTORAL PRIORITY AND COMPARATIVE
     ADVANTAGE

In Chapter 10 we outlined a method of identifying the pattern of comparative advantage for the society in planning its produc- tion. The basic idea is to take advantage of the possibility of trade with other nations, to make the goods that the society can produce at relatively low cost (i.e. relative to that in other nations) and to import, in exchange for some of its produce, the goods that it can make only at a relatively high social cost.

Although the principle sounds as if it would appeal to common sense, there have been strong objections to it both in theory and in practice.

At least two kinds of arguments are encountered in favour of a much more autarkic growth strategy than is suggested by the criterion of comparative advantage. The first kind, originating in the Soviet development strategy, has since been transformed into an orthodoxy of socialist planning.[1] The argument in the context of Soviet planning was that it would be naïve and dangerous to specialise on the basis of comparative advantage calculations when the industrial countries could not be relied upon for supplies. Thus whatever the dictates of such calculations, sufficient domestic capacity must be built in all 'basic industries', particularly capital goods and strategic materials.

The doctrine undoubtedly made sense during the earlier phase of Soviet industrialisation since it was very much a solitary nation surrounded by actually or potentially hostile nations. Also its massive size in the long run provided a safeguard against uneconomic scales and thereby limited the cost of autarky to the society. In a real sense, it was not a rejection of the criterion of comparative advantage, but an acknowledgment that the major assumption of the theory that supplies can be obtained from abroad at the costs at which goods were produced abroad did not apply. What is, however, difficult to justify is the survival of the doctrine to this day as a model for every developing country. Whatever the ideological colours of a developing nation in the contemporary world, it can always be assured of enough nations willing to trade to make sensible specialisation profit-

[1] It may be noted that in the Soviet Union itself the strategy was extensively debated. There were many (e.g. Shanin, the head of the State Bank) who argued for continued long-run trading relations with the industrial countries based on the Soviet export of low-cost products (mainly agricultural goods) and import of industrial goods, chiefly machines. Others argued that the inevitable initial import of machines must be used to expand rapidly the domestic capacity in capital goods irrespective of relative costs because dependence on the capitalist countries for such supplies was dangerous and should be terminated as soon as possible. The latter doctrine prevailed not because of any ideological orthodoxy inherent in the classical Marxian theory but because of the realistic assessment of practical considerations. See Alec Nove, *An Economic History of the U.S.S.R.* (Allen Lane, The Penguin Press, 1969), Chapter 5, for a summary discussion and further references.

able. Needless to say that in the kind of calculations described above, the impossibility of trade with specific countries and in specific goods can easily be allowed for.

The second kind of argument, originating perhaps in the context of Indian planning during the fifties, is based on the idea of 'export pessimism' for the developing nations. It is argued that the comparative advantage calculations are not of much use in a situation of inelastic world demand for the goods that such calculations show to be profitable exports. Thus to balance external trade, import substitution must be extended to those sectors also in which there does not appear to be any cost advantage at present. Particularly important is to create domestic capacity in the capital goods industries whose output would determine the rate of investment and growth in the situation of stagnant exports.

Once again, if the export pessimism is real, the incremental pattern of comparative advantage can be made to reflect its effects. Thus in terms of our model in Chapter 10, if we think that the demand for existing exports is inelastic, we can make necessary allowances by adjusting the marginal export revenue downward according to the estimated value of the elasticity in the relevant range. The result will be to make otherwise relatively more expensive sectors profitable enough for domestic production and export through a reduction in the social rate of return. The trade gap will tend to close due both to import substitution and export expansion.[1]

The usual response, however, is to conclude from a supposed export pessimism that comparative advantage calculations are quite useless and to adopt policies designed to promote import substitution in undesirable directions through distortions in incentives. These policies often discriminate against exports and provide *ex post* 'proof' for the doctrine of export pessimism. A more reasonable alternative would be to take into account the real export prospects and obtain the benefit of the trading possibilities that exist.

One important point to note from the results of Chapter 10 is that in deciding sectoral priorities it does not make much sense to talk in terms of broad groups like capital goods and consumption

---

[1] See Chapter 10 for a discussion of the mechanism.

goods in the way it has been done in the literature on development planning. Our calculations show that most of the capital goods sectors are profitable enough to deserve domestic production, while consumption goods like paper and synthetic textiles are so costly to produce as to make imports more attractive. Admittedly, the result is partly due to the existing and immediately predictable output composition of the sectors, and for industries like machinery with small domestic capacity, it could change in future. What is interesting to note, however, is that the 'heavy industry' of basic metals, represented in the model largely by the input structure of a rather uneconomically small modern steel plant, proves socially profitable while the products of consumption goods industries like sugar, paper and rayon, purported to be processing indigenous raw materials, are required to be imported. Whether a commodity should be produced or not depends on how intensively it uses scarce inputs in relation to the prices at which they can be imported from abroad. Many of the capital goods, despite being labelled 'heavy industries', come out better on this test.

12.5 IMPLEMENTING SECTORAL PLANS

The process of industrial planning can be described as a sequence of the following decisions although, strictly speaking the decisions are simultaneous rather than sequential. It ought to begin with the identification of the broad pattern of social comparative advantage from which will emerge the pattern of sectoral priority in investment allocation. The next step is to identify the sectors and products requiring bulky investment and capacity expansion on a large-scale. Since the public sector will have to play the overwhelming role in these parts, its investment programme will have to be formulated accordingly. This will define the area of activity of the private sector, the remaining few large-scale industries in which it might reasonably hope to operate in view of its limited resources, and the small-scale industries.

Why should it be necessary to plan, to identify the pattern of sectoral priorities from the detailed calculation of social costs? The answer lies in the well-known phenomenon that the market does not reflect social scarcities even remotely. This is partly because Bangladesh has inherited a relative price structure which is the reflection of a large number of arbitrary controls instituted in the past. It will take time to rationalise the controls and for the price and production structure to adjust, even if the policymakers intend to do so. Some of the distortions in the market are, of course, due to inherent factors and will continue to be reflected in market prices even when grossly non-uniform controls resulting in non-uniform incentives for various sectors are removed. The cases of externalities, infant industries and income distribution are well-known and need no explanation. There is also the important consideration that market wages are higher than the social cost of labour, whatever sensible objectives and assumptions may underlie the calculations.

Unless some attempt is made to make systematic corrections in these directions, it would be impossible to identify a socially desirable pattern of sectoral output capacities. In Chapter 10 we outlined a general equilibrium method of making such corrections. In actual planning, solutions will be required on a much more detailed basis. Either the model will have to be applied to a far more detailed sector classification scheme or a good deal of additional information will have to be combined with the results of a somewhat aggregated application of the model.

The public sector investment allocation could follow the pattern of sectoral priorities once they are known. Even if the market profits are different from the relative social profits generated by the sectors, there would be no compelling reason for the public sector to be guided by the former. However, the problem of financing can easily become a bottleneck if market profits are systematically lower than social profits in all or most sectors of Goverment operation. Also, it is worth while to note that in the past the public sector enterprises were no less victims of the illusion of market prices than was the private sector. Unless a clearly defined method of evaluating investment projects is designed and applied in all public sector undertakings there is every likelihood that behaviour in future will be no different.

For the private sector, mere knowledge of the socially profitable sectors will not be enough. Unless actual market profits are made at least approximately proportional to social profits, the private sector cannot be made to undertake the socially desirable

investments. The kind of factors that will make private calculations different from the social ones have been mentioned
above. A beginning must be made by rationalising the relative
price structure through reducing and making uniform the rates
of protection. With infant industries and externalities, the main
problem is one of identification; unless the presence of these
factors is clearly identified, there would be little benefit from
ad hoc actions based on unsubstantiated presumptions.

About one factor, however, there would be little doubt. Private industry will be paying a higher price for labour than the
social cost of employment. In the past, its effect on the rate of
profit was more than offset in most manufacturing industries by
high effective protection and the underpricing of capital and its
wasteful effect was reflected in the extremely high capital-
intensity of the techniques chosen in manufacturing industries.
If in future effective protection and underpricing of capital are
rendered negligible, the fact that the market wage is higher than
labour's social cost will mean that the market rate of profit in
manufacturing will be lower than the social rate. In the more
likely case of significant (but hopefully not overt) effective protection, the rate of profit would probably be high enough to
reflect true social profitability, but the relative overpricing of
labour would shift private incentives away from the relatively
more labour-intensive techniques and would generally lead to
a misallocation of resources. Some compensatory action would
then be called for.

One way of introducing such compensatory action would be
to provide the private sector with a wage subsidy.[1] In fact such
a subsidy can be used as a more general weapon of directing
private investment and providing 'protection' to deserving
industries. Since our calculations in Chapter 6 show an unmis-
takable social advantage for small-scale techniques, and since it
is likely that the private sector will continue to suffer for quite
some time in future from its habit of thought acquired under
an irrational incentive system strongly preferring large-scale
enterprises, it would make sense to confine such a subsidy to the
private small-scale sector only. This would help achieve the

---

[1] A proposal for wage subsidy, as a general means of promoting industries
as opposed to protecting them, is to be found in Little, Scott and Scitovsky,
op. cit.

objective of directing private investment in the socially desirable direction.

The feasibility of such a policy has been challenged on the ground that it would be difficult to finance. The argument, on examination, seems quite baseless. We have seen in Chapter 10 that on quite plausible assumptions, the shadow wage *ratio* would be high, perhaps no less than seven-eighths of the value of workers' consumption. The value of workers' consumption itself would be less than at market prices. We hope, however, that product prices would tend to get closer to social scarcities in future due to the general reduction in the level of protection. Thus a 15 to 20 per cent wage subsidy would go a long way to offset the effect of the difference between market and social costs of labour.

The share of wages in value added is about 40 per cent (except in those large capital-intensive industries which are likely to be under the public sector and where the share is lower) and in gross value of output around 20 per cent. Thus an industry-wide wage subsidy of 20 per cent can be financed by a 4 per cent additional indirect tax on the value of output. But such a sub-sidy would be given only to the private sector and small-scale enterprises while the base of the indirect tax would include, apart from total industrial and some non-industrial output, imports. It would, therefore seem that not much more than an additional 1 per cent of indirect taxation on all manufactured and imported goods would be necessary to finance a 20 per cent wage subsidy to private small-scale industries.

The benefits from such a policy would be considerable. The choice of technique would tend towards the socially desirable one. The private sector would have the proper incentive to go where it ought to, the small-scale manufacturing enterprises and the problem of employment would be easier to handle.

12.6 PRIVATE FOREIGN INVESTMENT

In the past private foreign investors were the beneficiaries of the policy of patronising industrial capitalists: the high effective protection provided them with a high rate of profit in terms of the domestic currency and the overvalued rate of exchange allowed them to repatriate their profit at a favourable rate. As they had long since ceased to be net capital importers as a group (profits being high enough to allow a reasonable rate of repatriation plus a moderate rate of internal expansion), the overvalued exchange rate did not hurt them; almost certainly it created a strong disincentive to bring in capital.

Usually there is a tendency in economic discussions to claim that the real benefit of private foreign investment far exceeds the value of the financial capital that comes in, that it brings in entrepreneurship and technology along with all the promise of the inflow of innovations in the latter. These arguments are used to justify special treatment to foreign capital.

What is, however, not known is the appropriateness of the technology imported by the private foreign investors. There is a considerable likelihood that their technology will at least partly be an imitation of that in the capital-exporting country, and therefore, largely inappropriate for the very different factor endowments of Bangladesh. The danger is that such technological distortions can easily spread through the demonstration effect to the domestically financed projects. Nor is it necessary for the demonstration effect to be limited to technology alone. It frequently extends to consumption and to high wage rates that are often offered to attract the best of the labour force.

Thus government policy towards private foreign investment has to be carefully determined. It should get none of the priviledges that we have argued should be denied to private domestic investors. Of the existing foreign enterprises, those which are clear drains on domestic resources through high net profit repatriation should be systematically made to behave in a socially more desirable way. The devaluation of the rate of exchange of the domestic currency should somewhat reduce the artificial incentive to repatriate profits rather than to reinvest. Stricter regulations through the revision of the repatriation entitlements may have to be resorted to if these measures fail.

13 Financing Development

13.1 SOME SPECIAL FEATURES

THE problem of generating an adequate surplus for a reasonable rate of investment is perhaps the most uncertain of all aspects of the economic future of Bangladesh. There is no obvious source of a large surplus that can be mopped up with relative ease. The size of the modern sector is small. Agriculture does not have the kind of extreme concentration of income and consumption in a few very rich households that can be observed in many pre-industrial economies. The vast agricultural sector is overwhelmingly a subsistence activity. Well over four-fifths of the economy is either unmonetised or based on a system of marketing and trade that cannot be taxed easily. The poor agricultural sector has only recently been subjected to rather heavy concealed taxation and can be made to pay for industrialisation once again only through the perpetuation of great inefficiency and inequity.

The cloud is not without a few silver linings, however. A very prominent one is to be found in the low defence burden which, though not automatically available under all possible circumstances, can be ensured by sensible external policies. Another bright aspect derives from the 'windfall' gain of the large part of the manufacturing industries deserted by their (West) Pakistani owners and taken over by the Government. Formerly their external ownership was a source of a large drain of resources, since much of their profit used to be repatriated. Now it can all augment public savings.

One unhealthy response to the circumstances consists of the pronouncement by members of the Government as well as friends abroad that Bangladesh cannot survive without massive foreign aid. To the extent that such pronouncements reduce the urgency of the admittedly difficult but necessary task of raising the rate of domestic surplus, they are of little help to economic

planning. In this chapter we shall try to make a realistic assessment of the resources that can be generated domestically and on
that basis try to estimate the necessary degree of dependence on
capital inflow.

13.2 DOMESTIC SAVINGS

13.2.1 *Public savings*

Our analysis in Chapter 9 showed that saving in the public
sector is likely to be quite high in comparison with what other
nations under similar circumstances have been able to achieve.
The main reasons are: (*a*) the existence of a tax structure imposed in the past by the central Pakistan Government which
can be made to generate a tax revenue of something around 8 to
9 per cent of GDP; (*b*) the ownership of the large-scale industrial enterprises deserted by (West) Pakistani industrialists and
businessmen which would be a source of surplus for the Government of Bangladesh; (*c*) the prospect of a very low outlay on
defence which claims well over half the revenue earnings of the
subcontinental governments; and (*d*) the freedom from the large
debt service that the former provincial Government in Dacca
was burdened with through a complicated accounting charade
devised by the then central Pakistan Government.

The investible surplus in the public sector, even without much
change in the tax structure[1] and with a generous allowance for
the vastly increased operation of the independent Government,
could be between 4 and 5 per cent of GDP under certain
reasonable assumptions (see Chapter 9). This would be radically
different from what the governments in most developing countries succeeded in achieving in recent times. The usual story is
one of insignificant revenue surplus and the financing of the
public sector programme by borrowing.

What are the prospects of increasing or diversifying the tax
revenue? The most important sources of revenue are customs
duty, excise duty and sales tax. A careful look at the pattern

---

[1] It is not being suggested that the inherited tax structure should be
retained intact. On the other hand, as is argued below, no great increase
in yield can be expected in the near future. The rationalisation of the tax
structure to achieve specific objectives could, of course, be attempted.

of these taxes suggests that it would be unrealistic to expect that their yield can be increased very much by increasing their rates in the short run. Significant expansion in their yield can only be obtained by the expansion in their bases, production in the organised sector of the economy and imports. There is one exception, however. If previous regional trade is successfully diverted to trade with the outside world (mostly with India in the short run), there would be an immediate increase in the base for customs and sales taxes through an expansion in imports. We have allowed for this possibility in our calculations in Chapter 9.

It might appear that customs revenue could be increased by mopping up some of the scarcity premium that used to be passed on to the licensed importers in the past. But the devaluation of the currency by a large margin (from about 11·5 to about 18·9 rupees to the pound sterling) has already reduced the scarcity premium considerably and we have argued against the policy of keeping the rate of exchange of the domestic currency overvalued.

The recent devaluation has been accompanied by an export tax on raw jute which should give a very large addition to revenue. We have not, however, included this in our calculations because we believe that this policy is wrong and ought to be abandoned in the interest of equalising the incentives for raw and manufactured jute and in the interest of long-term survival of jute as an important foreign exchange earner.

In the total tax revenue, the share of direct income and corporation taxes is fairly low, probably no more than 15 per cent. Some scope for advance exists in the possible extension of the existing rates to non-salary incomes, particularly those of the urban professionals. But no dramatic increase is likely. In the short run the likely effect is that of a reduction in the revenue from income tax because of the income limits imposed on both public and private sector salaries on an *ad hoc* basis. But this will not worsen the financial situation of the Government. For the public sector this merely means a 100 per cent tax beyond some income limit. For the private sector the lost income tax revenue should be made up by the increased yield from profits tax.

Thus, while the consolidation of the existing taxes and their proper enforcement will provide the Government with quite a high rate of public saving, due to certain structural advantages, it does not appear easy to obtain a rapid increase in public savings in the near future. Great importance should, therefore, be attached to the objective of maintaining the current advantage and in using the existing surplus to obtain maximum benefit in terms of expansion in productive capacity.

13.2.2 *Generating a surplus in agriculture*

The question of generating a surplus in agriculture will have to be approached with great caution. In the recent past, the sector's direct contribution to public revenue has amounted to Rs. 150 million of land revenue and Rs. 18 million of agricultural income tax. These are respectively 6·5 per cent and 0·8 per cent of the estimated total tax revenue that was raised in Bangladesh during the corresponding period by the Central and Provincial Governments. The incidence of concealed indirect taxation has been much higher.

We have already noted the importance of rejecting the strategy of another spell of 'primitive accumulation' from agriculture to finance the industrialisation of Bangladesh.[1] Only recently has such accumulation been carried out in Bangladesh agriculture to finance the industrialisation programme in West Pakistan and to a much lesser extent in Bangladesh itself, largely under West Pakistani ownership. The repetition of the

---

[1] Eugene Preobrazhensky, during the Soviet industrialisation debates in the twenties, coined the term 'primitive socialist accumulation' as a parallel to Marx's concept of 'primitive capitalist accumulation' to describe the process of initial capital accumulation in a pre-industrial economy attempting socialist industrialisation. He argued that such accumulation must be made from the private sector, which largely meant agriculture (apart from the small private capitalist sector operating under the New Economic Policy). He realised that such a surplus cannot be obtained voluntarily or even by taxation. He therefore argued for the exploitation of private agriculture through 'unequal exchange', i.e. by the Government, the monopoly supplier of manufactured and imported goods, turning the terms of trade against agriculture through decreed prices. Although Preobrazhensky was rejected in his time, Soviet industrialisation strategy later was based very much along the lines suggested by him. We use the term in the Preobrazhensky sense, except that we omit the word 'socialist'; in the case of Bengal his technique was adopted to generate surplus to finance capitalist industrialisation in West Pakistan.

process so soon would have disastrous consequences for agricultural growth.

On the other hand, the economy can never hope to attain a reasonable overall rate of investment without agriculture saving at least at a moderate rate. The answer would appear to lie in diverting the surplus generated in agriculture to finance the investment needs of the sector itself and to establish a clear and identifiable link between the source of saving and the location of investment.

Part of this can be achieved by the kind of policy outlined in Chapter 11. Most of the farmers are too small to be able to plan and finance investment projects on their own. In the absence of sufficiently divisible and profitable investment packages, the saving they might have done could easily get dissipated into consumption. Much of the saving of the small peasants would depend on the form and availability of sufficiently divisible investment packages. It is also likely that the act of saving will have to be 'financed' in the case of many small peasants by the provision of working capital by public sector agencies. Thus many peasants will be able to pay for the investment only when output is available, although the time lag is likely to be very short.

With policies like these, it should be possible to get the agricultural sector to save at a reasonable rate in an average crop year. We have too little behavioural information to be able to make any confident quantitative forecast, but the saving rate should be fairly elastic with respect to the policy package. In a normal crop year, the Government could reasonably aim at achieving, say, a more than 8 per cent saving rate (which would be between 4 and 5 per cent of GDP). We have seen that in a good crop year, despite very unfavourable government policies, the farmers saved 12 per cent of their current income in 1963/64. Although a single year's evidence is not much to go upon, there is little counter-evidence to suggest that a more modest result cannot be achieved with far more favourable policies.

Voluntary saving, though overwhelmingly important, should not be the only contribution of agriculture to national capital formation. Even if capital accumulated in agriculture is not used for investment elsewhere, there would be the need to finance the public sector's overhead investment in agriculture. It would be unreasonable to expect that the past trend can be completely reversed by getting the surplus generated by the non-agricultural sectors to finance such investment in agriculture (except, perhaps, for multi-purpose projects like flood control for which even some external resource might be sought). Thus agriculture will have to make some contribution to public revenue as well.

It would be better to achieve this with the help of a simple and direct tax if possible. The 'concealed' and indirect methods of the past both create a great many additional distortions as well as making it impossible to know the actual extent of surplus generation that the sector is being subjected to. This brings us to a dilemma in the problem of development finance. There does not seem to be any simple and profitable way of taxing subsistence agriculture.

The difficulty is inherent in the ownership pattern. The average farmer paying land tax is too small, making too little a payment in tax revenue. The collection cost per unit of tax is thus high. Also the rate of land tax cannot be very high in view of the extreme poverty of the average farmer.

It has sometimes been argued that the net yield of land revenue is so little that it should be abolished altogether. In 1969/70, land revenue in Bangladesh was estimated to be Rs.150 million while the expenditure on the Government's revenue department was Rs. 99 million.[1] Such an argument would strengthen the desire to redeem the promise of the ruling political party that all holdings below 8·3 acres (25 *bighas*) would be exempted from land revenue. If a land reform along the lines suggested in Chapter 11 is implemented, this would amount to the abolition of land revenue. Even with the present distribution of ownership, such an exemption would reduce the yield of land revenue to less than a third.

The argument that the net revenue from land tax is only a third of gross revenue seems to be fallacious. Much of the revenue department will have to be maintained as long as land records, ownership transfers and the related practices survive. In other words, the marginal cost of land revenue collection is

[1] Planning Department, *East Pakistan Economic Survey 1969–70* (Dacca, June 1970). These figures are estimates for 1969/70.

far less than the total expenditure on the revenue department. A decision to abolish land revenue would mean the decision to give up something closer to Rs. 150 million annually rather than a mere Rs. 50 million. Unless some alternative method of taxing agriculture is found, it would be a thing that the Government could ill-afford to give up.

Any alternative method of taxation under the conditions of highly dispersed peasant farming would both be expensive to collect and difficult to organise. There are instances of indirect taxes on output in underdeveloped agriculture in some socialist countries, but this is possible because of collective or co-operative farming which has far fewer points of collection. Thus, at the moment it is difficult to find a reasonable alternative to land revenue. It would, of course, be desirable to simplify and rationalise the tax so as to introduce a certain amount of flexibility and progressivity in the system by periodic adjustments in the rate to reflect the results of the Government's development programme on the yield per acre and by having a slightly higher rate for each subsequent acre beyond the average size.

What is important to realise is that in the past agriculture suffered not so much from land revenue, but mainly because of the massive disincentives and concealed taxes built into the exchange rate and fiscal system. If the farmers had been offered a slightly less unfavourable exchange rate for their jute exports, its effect could have more than offset that of land revenue. The removal of these disincentives and the inputs and credit programme by the public sector agencies should increase the taxable capacity of agriculture substantially. It would only be fair to mop up a bit of the increased real income of the farmers to finance the overhead programmes in agriculture.

13.2.3 *Savings in the non-agricultural sectors*

Only a small part of the non-agricultural sectors could be counted as a tax base. Much of the cottage industries, traditional transport and trade and services are purely subsistence activities and would remain outside the scope of any taxation programme in the near future. Their savings behaviour would perhaps be similar to that of the subsistence farmers. Under appropriate policies, it may be possible to get them to save at a modest rate, although it would serve little useful purpose to speculate on the likely magnitude of such an effort.

The sectors that are expected to contribute to both public revenue and private capital formation would be manufacturing industries, banking, insurance, organised trade, modern transport and urban professional services. Their total share in GDP is small, no greater than 15 per cent. Assuming that the share of pre-tax gross profits in value added is about half and that the recent saving rate (about 50 per cent) obtaining in the corporate sector of the former state of Pakistan would apply to these sectors, their contribution to private capital accumulation can be over 3 per cent of GDP.[1]

We can, of course, hardly feel confident about these estimates. We are applying the savings behaviour of a rather different group to this heterogeneous group with unknown saving propensities. Balanced against this is the consideration that a good deal of the potential surplus in the corporate business sector was dissipated into the consumption of business executives and capitalists under the old tax laws which allowed many such items to be charged as business costs. These included luxury housing, cars, personal service, unlimited entertainment and luxury travel and a wide range of durable consumption goods. Even recognising that the price of private enterprise must be paid in terms of higher consumption by the capitalists, there would be no justification to go to such an extent. Tax laws could be suitably changed to reduce, if not completely abolish, the permissible items of such consumption that can be charged as business costs.

It may be useful to discuss briefly the role of financial institutions in mobilising savings. In the past, the return on savings

---

[1] The share of gross pre-tax profits in value-added has been above 65 per cent in manufacturing but possibly lower elsewhere. We estimate the average, somewhat arbitrarily but plausibly, to be 60 per cent. Reinvestment of gross profits in the corporate sector of the former Pakistan was found to be just over 50 per cent by Baqai and Haq, 'Savings and Financial Flows in the Corporate Sector, 1959–63', the *Pakistan Development Review*, autumn 1967. Combining these we find the sectors' contribution to capital formation to be over 4·5 per cent of GDP. We, however, subtract 1·5 percentage points to avoid double counting of the saving by the public sector manufacturing enterprises which has already been included in the public saving estimate.

invested in the commercial banks and other saving institutions was very low. Allowing for the rise in the general level of prices, the real rates of interest on bank deposits during the nineteen-sixties were found to be highly negative.[1] In this situation, as Nuruddin Chowdhury comments, 'not saving is the surest way to avoid income losses. . . . Saving propensities of spending units in the economy are depressed. . . . Even the savings that take place are channelled to acquisition of less productive forms of real assets to avoid the loss due to inflation. The amount released for real investment tends to be lowered even more.'[2]

The main reason behind this was the oligopolistic banking structure, owned by the (West) Pakistani industrial oligarchs who wanted to ensure the supply of loans to the industries under their control at very low rates of interest. The public sector actively encouraged this by getting the few publicly owned banks to follow the same policy and by making the Central Bank (the State Bank of Pakistan) impose direct restrictions on price competition (i.e. competition in offering higher interest rates to attract more deposits). The ostensible purpose was to keep the incentive to invest high!

The spending units cannot be expected to abstain from consumption in the socially desired degree if the return on their saving has no correspondence to the scarcity price of capital. The real return on deposits in financial institutions must be made reasonable if potential savings are not to be dissipated in consumption or 'investment' in unproductive assets.

The breakdown of the private oligopoly of the banking system should be a help in achieving the required change in policy. Due to the circumstances of independence the Government of Bangladesh finds itself the owner of all the giants among the financial institutions. The few small institutions owned by Bengali financial groups are also due for nationalisation if the ruling party redeems its promise. What must be remembered is that nationalisation by itself is likely to do little social good unless the policy of providing cheap credit to 'favoured clients' at the cost of small or negative returns to actual savers is replaced by a

[1] Nuruddin Chowdhury in his paper on 'Income Redistributive Intermediation in Pakistan' in the *Pakistan Development Review*, summer 1969, estimates the real rates to be $-4 \cdot 07$, $-2 \cdot 22$, $-9 \cdot 25$ and $+3 \cdot 12$ per cent for each successive year beginning in 1964/65.   [2] Ibid.

more sensible one of making the price of credit and deposit rates reflect their much higher social values.

To summarise, in a normal year and under appropriate policies Bangladesh should be able to generate enough domestic savings to finance an investment programme of 11 to 12 per cent of GDP. If the past capital-output ratios are any guide to what these may be in future, the economy should be able to generate $4\frac{1}{2}$ per cent annual growth on the basis of domestic saving alone.[1] By opting for less capital-intensive and small-scale industries to a much greater extent than in the past, the rate of growth may be raised above 5 per cent from internal savings. This is far from a pessimistic prognosis. On the other hand, there is nothing automatic or deterministic about it; its achievement will be dependent on the adoption of appropriate policies.

13.3 FOREIGN EXCHANGE AND AID

If by a combination of appropriate policies and average circumstances with respect to the natural factors a reasonably high rate of domestic saving can be achieved, can the supply of foreign exchange be increased to the required extent to translate the savings into actual investment? The basic mechanism can be demonstrated through the model outlined in Chapter 10. If the elasticity of demand for the primary exports like jute and tea is not high, additional exports must be found and imports economised through substitution by domestic production along more and more socially costly sectors. The external account can of course always be balanced by continuing until enough exports and import substitutes are produced, exchange rate adjusted and the social rate of return in the economy driven down.

When external borrowing is possible, it would not make sense to go on indefinitely along the process indicated. If at any given social rate of return (r_o) the foreign exchange gap $(M_o - X_o)$ can be met by borrowing the required quantity in the international

---

[1] The incremental capital-output ratio for the Bangladesh economy during 1970/75 was estimated from a multisectoral exercise by the present author to be just over 2 (see his article 'The Possibilities of the East Pakistan Economy during the Fourth Plan', the *Pakistan Development Review*, summer 1969).

Since investment in such calculations was net of depreciation, a modest rate of allowance for it has been made in calculating the rate of growth.

market at a rate of interest less than the social rate of return, then it would pay to borrow rather than trying to bridge the gap by export expansion and/or import substitution through a reduction in the social rate of return (see the diagram). The assumption implied is that the socially optimal use of foreign borrowing (and capital generally) will be made so that the return on them will be as high as r_o.

From this standpoint, it would appear that much of the borrowing in the past (during the partnership with Pakistan) did not make sense. The nominal rate of interest on a good deal of borrowing has in recent years been 6 per cent or more and we shall see that the effective rate of interest may have been much higher. Against this, we find that the social rate of return in many sectors has been lower than 6 per cent, sectors which probably would not have been expanded except for the availability of foreign capital (see Table 10.5 in Chapter 10).

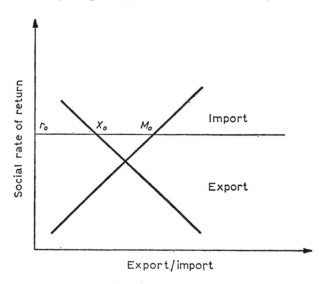

market at a rate of interest less than the social rate of return, then it would pay to borrow rather than trying to bridge the

What guidelines do we derive for future policy toward foreign borrowing? As we found in Chapter 10, the social rate of return for the Bangladesh economy is probably of the order of magnitude of 16 per cent. Admittedly, one should not make too much out of the numerical estimation made on the basis of the past production structure with imperfect data, but there is no obvious reason to suppose that the social rate of return would be very much higher. This means that if the economy is operating on the efficiency frontier and making the optimum use of resources, then it would pay to borrow at rates of interest below 16 per cent.

In actual practice the limit would almost certainly be somewhat lower than 16 per cent, perhaps around 12 per cent or so, to allow for the various administrative costs and uncertainties. Although it may not be obvious, this is quite a low ceiling and would certainly require a careful check on the available loan offers. To begin with, it is well known that the widespread phenomenon of foreign aid 'tied' to a particular source of purchase often means a higher price of aid-financed equipment. Empirical evidence has shown that a 50 per cent higher price is quite common while a price up to 100 per cent higher is not an unknown phenomenon.[1] Depending on the pattern of repayment, even a 50 per cent higher price may mean nearly twice as high an effective interest rate, as compared to the nominal one.

Tying can increase the cost of aid in other ways also. Because of tying, Bangladesh may be forced to buy equipment in the U.S.A. market which is designed for the factor proportions of most capital-rich economy in the world while the socially desirable technique is perhaps incorporated in the equipment designed, for example, in Japan, China or India to suit a relatively more labour-abundant economy. The very act of such borrowing will force the economy to operate *within* and not *on* the efficiency frontier.

Add to this the general possibility that in spite of fairly enlightened and sincere policies, the economy will operate somewhat within the efficiency frontier. In these circumstances it will no longer make sense to contract many of the 6 to 8 per cent nominal interest bearing loans.

We have, of course, been assuming that future policy makers will be sensible enough to want to borrow only to supplement domestic resources and not, as often has been argued quite convincingly to have been the case, to replace them; we assume that foreign aid is not going to be used to create the illusion of

[1] See John Adler (editor), *Capital Movements and Economic Development* (Macmillan, 1967), especially the article by Mahbub-ul Haq.

abundance of foreign exchange to encourage its underpricing to privileged users. If these possibilities are recognised to be real dangers, then one would want to discount the probable benefits of foreign aid even more and settle for an even lower cut-off interest rate.[1]

The discussion above should provide some sobering thought to those in Bangladesh whose first reaction on independence has been to look for foreign borrowing. This reaction is unhealthy and is warranted neither by the conditions of what foreign aid might achieve, nor by what the economy can perform by way of domestic resource generation. To be sure, foreign aid can be of use and will almost certainly have to be resorted to in order to accelerate growth and to remove various specific bottlenecks. But a critical evaluation must continuously be made about the benefit and cost to the society accruing from each act of borrowing.

Once again the experience of Pakistan should serve as the basis for education. It was argued that foreign aid would pay for itself because of its high productivity in terms of output and exports. By 1970, the country, faced with a sharply rising ratio of debt service to foreign exchange earnings, had joined the long queue of nations seeking a moratorium on and re-scheduling of foreign debt. The argument that the difficulty was due to the political turmoil that ultimately led to the emergence of Bangladesh is not at all convincing. Even before the troubles, by July 1970, the outstanding indebtedness had reached $3149 million or nearly five times the exports of the then Pakistan. The debt service for 1970/71 was to be $216 million or nearly a third of export earnings.[2] Long before the direct confrontation had started on Bangladesh, Pakistan had joined the rank of the defaulters on aid repayment.

If Bangladesh does anything like Pakistan did during the fifties and sixties, the consequences would be worse. This is

---

[1] Although no definite proof of the direction of causation can be established, the strong negative correlation between the domestic saving rate and the rate of capital inflow is disturbing. See Anisur Rahman, 'Foreign Capital and Domestic Savings: A Test of Haavelmo's hypothesis with Cross Country Data', *Review of Economics and Statistics*, 1968.

[2] The figures are from: Government of Pakistan, Ministry of Finance, *Pakistan Economic Survey, 1970–71* (Islamabad, June 1971).

because of the steadily declining share of grants in total capital inflow and the worsening terms of borrowing over time. During the period 1950–5, nearly 68 per cent of Pakistan's foreign capital inflow consisted of grants; during 1965–70, the share had fallen to a mere 6 per cent.[1]

The basic policy requirements and main directions for exports have been outlined respectively in Chapters 8 and 10. A significant step towards the dismantling of the hopelessly complicated and non-uniform multiple exchange rates set up under Pakistan's export bonus scheme and its substitution by a more realistic and uniform rate of exchange has already been taken. The rupee has been devalued from about 11·5 to about 18·9 to the pound sterling. With regard to the policies concerning the major export, raw jute, the hangover from the past seems to have survived, however. Much of the effect of the devaluation has been offset in the case of raw jute by the simultaneous imposition of an export tax, according to the available reports. We have argued at length in Chapter 8 that the underlying idea behind such a policy, namely, that the world demand for Bangladesh jute is inelastic, is based on serious misjudgements and misconceptions. Much of the devaluation should have been passed on to the importers abroad and the cultivators at home. This would be the only way to halt the trend of the declining share of Bangladesh jute in the total jute/kenaf export market and reverse it in the long-run.

After jute, tea is the next major commodity in which Bangladesh has an export surplus created by the cessation of trade with Pakistan. Immediate negotiation should be started to recover the traditional market in the U.K. that was lost in the early sixties due to the forcible direction of exports to (the then West) Pakistan. There should not be any serious glut in the world export market as a result of the entry of Bangladesh as a supplier since Pakistan has already entered the market as a buyer.[2]

Jute manufactures, even after equalising the incentive for them with that for raw jute, should be profitable enough for

[1] Ibid.

[2] The task of getting back the traditional U.K. market may be made easier by the fact of large-scale British ownership of the tea plantations in Bangladesh. This might be regarded as the redeeming feature of the Government decision not to nationalise these plantations.

exports if our calculations are right. Further capacity and export expansion should be co-ordinated with the Indian plans along these lines, preferably in the context of a general agreement on the specialisation and sharing of respectively the production of raw jute and the export of jute manufactures.

We have noted that expansion of capacity in paper would be socially unprofitable unless a much more favourable production technique is available. We have, however, noted that the continued utilisation of the existing capacity will almost certainly be desirable as the massive capital stock will have little alternative value and should properly be regarded as zero-cost assets in deciding whether to keep operating the existing capacity or not. This means that Bangladesh will have some considerable export surplus of paper arising out of the cessation of trade with Pakistan. It may be quite easy to find an alternative market in view of the large net import into India at the moment. Growing trade between the two countries will certainly make it possible to have this surplus absorbed in India at some reasonable price. In case of the other important commodity, matches, the alternative source of absorption is not all that clear and may involve quite a bit of looking around.

In what direction should additional exports be sought? The model in Chapter 10 throws up leather and leather products as a particularly profitable export commodity. In the recent past Pakistan had a remarkable growth in leather exports and even Bangladesh had some share in this either directly or through increased export of leather to (West) Pakistan. By diversifying the product and standardising and improving quality, very significant expansion may be possible in this direction.

The other likely expansion in exports would be in fishery, an activity shrouded in the residual conglomeration of 'other agriculture, forestry and fishery' in the sector classification scheme adopted in the application of the model in Chapter 10. Neither in leather, nor in fishery would there be an adequate volume of ready export surplus over the existing quantities of export; expansion in production capacity will have to be brought about through investment in these sectors to generate such a surplus.

Beyond these not much can be seen with clarity and the success of vision would appear to depend on very detailed investigations. But export revenue from the above goods and the small bits of the many smaller existing exports could be quite large, especially if appropriate policies are adopted with respect to jute. With successful import substitution in the production of grain, the above exports should provide a big enough foreign exchange revenue to enable the economy to depend only modestly on foreign assistance.

14 Prospects of Short-term Transition and Long-term Growth: Some Concluding Remarks

14.1 SHORT-TERM TRANSITION

A summary view of the divergent elements of the arguments developed in the preceding chapters is now necessary. This may be attempted by trying to answer in the light of the above discussion the question we asked at the outset: Will Bangladesh emerge as a viable nation which would be able to solve both the short-term problem of transition and the long-term problem of growth? Or will the 72 million people continue to sink deeper into a huge morass of poverty and chaos?

It should be clear from the above discussion that no deterministic prediction can be made about the future of Bangladesh. The outcome essentially depends on the policies pursued by and the organisational ability of the political leadership. The problems are so acute and extensive that they would be a formidable challenge to even the most brilliant and well-organised political machinery. The huge burden of population and the rapid rate of its increase, the acuteness of poverty, hunger, disease and ignorance would be considered unprecedented even under 'normal' circumstances. There also exist purely technical problems of a massive scale, e.g. that of controlling floods. All these extreme problems have to be tackled by a society which has too few resources and too little margin of surplus above subsistence consumption.

The problems have been greatly compounded in the short run because of the violent transition leading to the nation's independence at the end of 1971. The need to resettle nearly ten million refugees, the growing shortage of food (estimated by the Government to be a staggering 2½ million tons during the twelve months beginning March 1972) due to the disruption in farming and the seriously damaged transport network are some of the features of the aggravation of the problem in the short-run.

In order to survive in the long run, the problem of transition will have to be overcome. However, from the standpoint of material resource requirements, the problem does not appear so serious. The large-scale industrial units could reach capacity output once some maintenance imports are made possible. This could be financed even by some short-term borrowing from abroad, since exports could begin with the resumption of industrial activity (and even before in the case of raw jute) which would help the economy to generate foreign exchange for future imports of raw materials. The disrupted transport network will be a problem, but not an insurmountable one. Already, the ports have been restored to working condition and the temporary use of the Indian port of Calcutta should not be ruled out as a possibility. Most of the smaller bridges were quickly put back to use and the hiring of water transport vehicles from abroad should begin to compensate for the reduced operation of rail and road transport. The food import requirement of $2\frac{1}{2}$ million tons seems to be an over-cautious estimate; it should be possible to obtain a reasonable winter (aman) harvest (which alone is normally 62 per cent of the total rice crop for the whole year) in November–December 1972 even if the tiny spring (boro) harvest and the small rainy season (aus) harvest are abnormally low.

The overwhelming limitation, however, seems to be management at all levels. The Government at the top, however well-intentioned, has no previous experience of running an administration. There was not a smooth transfer of power, and consequently the nation was deprived of the assets of the overthrown régime. In addition, the middle class composition of the government and their conventional methods of operation seriously limit the range of feasible policies. Although the nation has gone through an unprecedented upheaval, there has been little grass-roots political organisation able to impose the necessary discipline on the unsettled population. The political upheaval and armed resistance continued long enough to make a serious dent in the confidence and respect of the people for the established structure of power, but the process did not last long enough for the emergence of an alternate structure.

Today the Government find themselves saddled with the responsibility of running a vast number of previously (West) Pakistani-owned and managed enterprises and they have few managerial resources to deploy. Their first act has been to appoint administrators to these enterprises. These administrators, however, do not appear to have much experience of management and their initial response has rarely gone beyond preparing a list of required materials and finance. There has really been very little initiative and improvisation at the plant level.

The same phenomenon is visible everywhere. The civil service is probably the only group with some semblance of organisation. But they too suffer from serious limitations. They have been trained as part of the Pakistan civil service in a framework of authoritarian government and hence are faced with the problem of adjusting to the very different circumstances of today. Moreover, they held too few top responsibilities in the past.

Considering these circumstances, it would be too much to hope that the Bangladesh economy can have a smooth and instantaneous transition to its pre-war level of industrial production. It is more likely that such a transition will be achieved gradually and at significant cost in terms of dislocation and loss of current output. The Government can, however, contribute by substituting determination for experience and by taking pragmatic decisions. In this context, they would be well advised to explore the possibility of importing managers for a specified short period if that is, as it indeed seems to be, the only way out of the present difficulties.

Another set of short-term problems is due to the need to adjust to the economic realities of the existence of the giant neighbour, India. Unlike in the past, the extraordinarily long and peaceful border with India will be impossible to police, partly because it would be beyond the capacity of the available army and police forces and partly because of the inevitable unpopularity of such measures. The relative price of the major agricultural goods, rice and jute among them, is lower in Bangladesh than in the neighbouring areas of India. There will be a tendency for smuggling out of rice, jute and other agricultural goods in exchange for manufactured consumer goods until the relative prices in Bangladesh approximate those in India more closely. This will create problems for the Bangladesh economy. Part of the problem will be due to the lower wage rates in Bangladesh as compared to wage rates in India. For example, wages in jute textiles in West Bengal are nearly 50 per cent higher than in Bangladesh. Thus it would mean a serious decline in the standard of living of the industrial wage-earners in Bangladesh if they were to absorb a level of food prices that face the much better paid workers across the border. Inevitably the upward adjustment of food prices will have to be offset somehow.

However, to try to stop such 'free trade' by trade restrictions would be a futile exercise. We have mentioned that it will be impossible to close the border without incurring a large economic and political cost. It will also be self-defeating to try to keep food prices low by increased imports. A much more sensible policy seems to be to recognise the reality and allow internal prices to adjust by having relatively free trade with India. This would mean the abolition of quantitative restrictions on trade and the adoption of a rate of tariff on imports not much higher than the rate of indirect taxes in India. This will take away the incentive to smuggle and at least ensure that the Government gets the customs revenue on imports. Otherwise, smuggling will ensure a revenue loss for the Government, since the smuggled outflows would be agricultural goods which are normally untaxed at the level of the production units, while the smuggled inflows would be manufactured goods on which taxes would be paid to the Indian Government.

The rise in food prices, resulting from relative free trading, will have to be offset in the short run by a direct consumption subsidy, in the form of cheaper rations for the low-income groups, for example (but certainly not by compulsory procurement of grains at lower prices). As wages gradually adjust in the long run, such measures could be withdrawn.

It might be pointed out that the recently imposed export tax on raw jute will be inconsistent with such policies. In fact, the export tax on raw jute will not work in any case short of the drastic and unpopular anti-smuggling measures like the banning of jute cultivation in the border belt and the policing of the boundaries with India.

It will of course not do to allow relative free trade with India with high protection with respect to the rest of the world. The Indian production structure has too many distortions to make it desirable for Bangladesh to have some sort of a 'customs union' with her through a high common external tariff.[1] It would make sense for Bangladesh to be a relatively free-trading nation with no more than a 30 to 35 per cent tariff[2] and insignificant dependence on quantitative restrictions on trade. The burden of adjustment will have to be borne by the rate of exchange and the Government should be prepared to devalue further if necessary.

An important aspect of our argument is that relative free trade with India will provide agriculture with badly needed incentives. It will mean a tremendous boost to jute production in particular and the virtual end of Indian jute cultivation. Thus India too will have a problem of adjustment, though of a smaller magnitude. The question therefore is not merely whether Bangladesh policymakers will find such policies convincing but also whether India would find such an adjustment acceptable.

14.2 LONG-TERM GROWTH

From a more long-term standpoint, the problems facing the Bangladesh economy would appear to be no less formidable. Not only is the average standard of living dismally low, but also the distribution of income is highly skewed; one particularly deplorable phenomenon of the distribution of income is the vast proportion of the labour force who are effectively unemployed and hence have little income. The annual addition to the population and labour force are by themselves staggering and this creates an enormous demand for resources.

Conventional industrialisation through protection and disproportionate and distorted incentives for private capitalists

[1] See Bhagwati, J., and P. Desai, *India: Planning for Industrialisation* (Oxford University Press, 1970) for a discussion of these distortions.

[2] This will not mean a reduction in customs revenue to any significant extent. The average rate of customs duty in the recent past has not been much more than 32 per cent of the value of imports. The effective tariff in the past has always been determined by quantitative restrictions.

will not be an answer to the problems. However rapidly industrialisation proceeds, it cannot absorb more than a fraction of even the increase in the labour force. It will also result in the standard wastes of protected industrialisation under sponsored private capitalism: wasteful use of scarce capital, inefficient production and undesirable concentration of income and wealth.

Except in those sectors where the considerations of technology or economies of scale dictate large-scale operation, industrialists should be induced to get rid of the past habit and undertake small-scale enterprises on a decentralised basis. On no account should incentives be distorted in favour of large-scale, capital-intensive techniques. Since our calculations pretty conclusively show that the small-scale techniques are usually socially more profitable, it might be a reasonable policy to induce private investors away from large-scale manufacturing into which private calculations and habits of thought will tend to push them.

The policy of discrimination against agriculture will have to be reversed and most of the surplus generated directly or indirectly in this sector should be used to finance investment therein. In view of the ruthless exploitation of this sector in the past, there is no other way of making it grow and save at a high marginal rate. The incentives to agriculture should be combined with a substantial redistribution of land ownership, particularly if a bi-modal kind of development leading to the increased proletarianisation of the small peasants is to be avoided.

Although there are many problems to be confronted, the rather favourable possibilities of the public sector achieving a high rate of saving is very encouraging. In this respect, much will depend on the ability of the Government to manage the currently owned public sector enterprises and to limit defence spending. None of these will be easy or automatic, but the failure to ensure success in either of these two directions would prove disastrous.

A responsible attitude towards external borrowing is an essential pre-requisite for success. Foreign borrowing should be sought only after the limits of domestic savings and exports are optimally explored and a loan should be contracted only after careful calculations show that its true costs are less than its social return. By adopting appropriate policies it should be possible to push the limits of domestic resources beyond what appears practicable from the past experience of inappropriate policies.

Finally, it must be recognised that with the existing rate of demographic increase, the burden of additional population will be nearly unbearable. Nor will the burden ease very much even if the past targets of population control were to be achieved. Such targets, set on the assumption that essential social and economic reforms could be avoided indefinitely, were necessarily unambitious and impotent. Appropriate priority must be assigned to this crucial objective by the political leadership and the necessary social and economic preconditions established. Dependence on the conventional programmes of mere exhortation will not bring about a demographic transition as quickly as is essential.

Given the determined implementation of such policies, Bangladesh should be able to pull out of the morass in which it seems to be at the moment. It is, however, far from certain that the political leadership will in fact be able or even willing to make such a clean break from the kind of economic policies pursued in the past by all the governments of the subcontinental nations.

Postscript

By June 1972, six months after independence, the economic policy of the Bangladesh Government has taken shape at least in outline. The most far-reaching institutional changes have taken place in the organised industrial and financial sectors. We have already noted that a very large proportion of enterprises, abandoned by the former (West) Pakistani owners, had been taken over by the Government immediately after independence. On 26 March 1972, the first anniversary of the declaration of independence, further measures were adopted. All jute and cotton textiles and sugar factories having Taka 1·5 million ($205 thousand at the official rate of exchange) or more of assets were nationalised. Simultaneously, it was decided that, of the abandoned enterprises, those having less than Taka 1·5 million of assets would be transferred to private or co-operative ownership.

The Bangladesh Industrial Development Corporation, the organisation through which the setting up and management of all public sector industries used to be undertaken, has been abolished. In its place ten sector corporations have been set up each to manage the nationalised and/or the abandoned enterprises in the relevant sector. The ten sectors are:

1. Jute Mills
2. Cotton Mills
3. Sugar Mills
4. Steel Mills
5. Paper and Board
6. Fertiliser, Chemical and Pharmaceutical
7. Engineering and Shipbuilding
8. Minerals, Oils and Gas
9. Food and Allied Products
10. Forest Products

It may be pointed out that the Government has taken over a very small number of enterprises with respect to which it had any option. The enterprises under sectors 4 to 10 above are those which had either already been under public ownership or been abandoned by the West Pakistanis. In sectors 1 to 3 a small proportion of the productive capacity belonged to the Bengali private owners and only with respect to these had the Government any real option. The rest had been under public ownership anyway.

Information is lacking about the precise extent of public ownership today. It has, however, been very crudely estimated that about 80 per cent of the assets in large-scale manufacturing industries have been nationalised. The remainder of the large-scale and medium and small-scale industries continue to be under private ownership.

Besides manufacturing industries, banks and insurance companies and jute export trade have been nationalised. Once again, a very high proportion of these enterprises had already been either under public ownership or taken over as abandoned property.

Nearly three months after nationalisation the physical take-over of the enterprises remains to be accomplished. The former managements, wherever present, have been asked to continue and administrators have been appointed in the abandoned ones. Thus private management still continues to operate three months after public ownership was decreed.

In June 1972 the principle of workers' participation in management was announced. It was decided that two of the five members of the management board for each nationalised enterprise will be elected by the workers.

Although the broad institutional framework for the nationalised enterprises had been worked out by June, the implementation of these measures had not yet begun at the enterprise level. Thus in a real sense the economy had yet to undergo the necessary institutional change. Much of the future potential of the economy will depend on the efficiency with which the necessary transformation is brought about. These industries, though together contributing a small proportion of the output produced by the economy, were a major source of surplus in the past. It is therefore of the utmost importance that the profitability of these enterprises survives their nationalisation. Otherwise the society will lose one of its few sources of reinvestible surplus.

The task does not seem to be an easy one. The former Industrial Development Corporation did not have a tradition of

high social efficiency so that the new sector corporations do not
have any given standard to live up to. There does not seem to be
any clear demarcation of responsibilities and powers between a
sector corporation and the constituent enterprises. Clearly a
period of experimentation will follow which is hardly likely to
guarantee efficiency during the period of transition. The
difficulties are compounded by the strong trend of syndicalism
prevalent among the dominant labour unions.

In terms of physical production the manufacturing industries
are gradually getting back to normal. The speed has varied
between sectors depending on the particular circumstances.
Thus jute textiles, insignificantly dependent on imported inputs,
attained 75 per cent of the daily output level prevalent in the
most recent normal year (1969–70) by the end of April. On the
other hand, cotton textiles, entirely dependent on imports for
raw materials, lagged behind.

The major dislocation that the economy has to cope with is
due to the cessation of supplies from (West) Pakistan, including
management. Alternative sources had to be identified. Ports
and the transport network had to be restored. New institutions
had to be set up. The process is still going on for many
industries.

The signs of the last year's war are most visible today in the
transport sector. Four major railway bridges still remain to be
repaired. Improvised services have been operating, but there
has been an increased delay in road and rail transport.

While the tiny organised sector of the economy underwent
major institutional changes during the first six months of
independence, the vast agricultural sector remained almost
completely untouched. The Government duly redeemed its
promise to abolish land revenue on all ownership units below
8·3 acres (25 bighas). This limit is nearly three and a quarter
times the average holding for an agricultural family in Bangladesh. For the moment the Government does not appear to
intend to carry out any significant land redistribution programme. Thus, the mammoth public meeting of 7 June,
organised by the ruling political party to listen to an important
policy speech by the Prime Minister, passed a resolution
'expressing satisfaction at the ceiling of highest holding of land
per family at 100 bighas and demanded distribution of surplus

land among the landless peasants free of cost'.[1] We have noted above that 100 bighas (33·3 acres) was the ownership ceiling imposed in the early fifties. Later on, some relaxation was provided if farmers wanted to mechanise, but less than 3 per cent of the total land is known to be held in ownership units larger than 100 bighas. It is, therefore, reasonably clear by now that the current thinking of the Government does not favour any further land reform.

Elsewhere the economy has been getting back to normal by gradual steps. By June the Bangladesh Bank (the central bank) had nearly completed the transition to a new currency, the Taka. The Bank had the unenviable task of floating a new currency without any reserves. By the end of May the gold and foreign exchange backing had risen to the respectable level of nearly 30 per cent of the actual currency in circulation. The Government depended very greatly on borrowing from the Bangladesh Bank to finance its expenditure during the first few months. This, however, does not seem to have generated much pressure of monetary demand because, according to all available indications, a good deal of currency flight took place immediately before independence.

Exports abroad had reached the monthly average of $24 million during March and April. This is nearly 90 per cent of the monthly average export abroad (except West Pakistan) during 1965–70 and nearly 70 per cent of the monthly average total export during the same period, valuing exports to West Pakistan at the present rate of exchange.

Foreign aid has started coming in. For the next fiscal year (July 1972 to June 1973) more than $400 million of foreign aid has either already been committed or is being definitely expected. It seems likely that the aid inflow may exceed $500 million during the next year with a very high proportion of grants. This is in complete contrast with the past and approaching the West Pakistan proportions during the sixties. Another point to note is that the United States has made enough aid commitments for the next year to emerge as by far the single largest aid donor. This is a considerably changed situation from the circumstances of the independence of Bangladesh which was

---

[1] *The Bangladesh Observer*, 8 June 1972, p. 8, col. 1.

supported by India and the U.S.S.R. and opposed by the United States.

To summarise: at the time of writing this postscript (June 1972) it appears likely that, with some exceptions, the major manufacturing industries of Bangladesh will achieve normal levels of output some time during the next fiscal year. Agriculture should have nearly a normal crop. A crash programme is being undertaken for agriculture in next year's development plan which will outweigh all the adverse effects of the recent disturbances. It is not unlikely, barring serious natural disaster, that grain output during the next fiscal year will approach or even exceed the peak output in recent years. The ambitious rehabilitation and reconstruction plan for the next year will not only fully restore but may also lead to some increase in economic infrastructural facilities like transport and communications. From the standpoint of economic organisation the large-scale manufacturing sector will have been overwhelmingly nationalised. So will the financial institutions and part of foreign trade. The vast rural sector will, however, experience little organisational and institutional change.

Index